THE SECRET TO BEING THANKFUL

Maverick Ashley Lenartson, Writer to the Stars "Keep Your Feet On The Ground, Keep Reaching For The Stars"- Casey Kasem

1001. You can go most anywhere you want anytime you want to.

1000. You can be friends with just about anyone who fits your cup of tea. Nobody says you have to befriend somebody who turns out to be a "passive aggressive ahole". Cut the ties before the two of you start arguing with each other all the time.

999. You have a right to not get a job. Get a disability check or go hungry and be forced to get a job that you hate. If you're going to get a job, then make sure it is something that you'd like to do that you'll be o.k. with 3 weeks down the road. You can always get a job doing something else until you find out what really floats your boat. Until then just hang in there.

998. You have a right to not pay your bills. Most people die hundreds of thousands of dollars in debt. That's just life: remember that you are E X P E N S I V E.

997. You can choose to live on the streets if you want to. I've done it before. I learned that it costs just as much to live on the streets as it does to be housed. So, stop being a pussy and make decisions that make things o.k. for you: this means getting anybody out of your life that keeps causing your problems and clearing up issues right away with people who don't do what they're supposed to do when they're supposed to do it: this includes roommates, lovers, employers, etc.

996. You can go back to school if you want to. You can do that at any point in your life. It's truly & totally up to you.

995. You can get your G.E.D. = General Education Degree

994. You can choose to eat only Vegetarian Food. Just remember that the hardest thing to digest is meat and that keeping white things out of your diet is a good thing to do: flour, dairy, sugar, junk food, etc. This doesn't mean that you can't cheat every now and then.

993. When somebody threatens you with violent words you can say, "Is that a threat of a good time?" They'll respond and say whatever they want to and you can say, "Hey, I'm not interested in you sexually so why don't we just end this right now."

992. If you are not a happy person, then the only person who can make you happy is YOU! Make a list of what things make you miserable and turn that around in your head:

991. You can choose to go hunting for red meat when you want to. Do you know what I'm saying: maybe you are sexually deprived or you just need more iron in your body.

990. You can choose to go fishing in a brook, lake, river or stream when you want to. Just make sure you have all the things you need to get the job done and that you've got your license to fish in the brook.

998. When somebody calls you about a bill that you owe you have a right not to pay that bill especially if the Debt Collector has been harassing you since you incurred the debt. In Maine, a debt does not have to be payed off after 6 years of being in Collections. Just make sure that you don't admit to owing the debt as it will go right back into collections and the Debt Collector will keep calling you and after 3 calls it's considered "harassment". Then you have the right to tell them to stop calling you and that this call is being logged in in my journal. Don't make debts that you can't afford to pay off: just make sure that you incur as little debt as possible with your life.

997. You can buy a car, a house or an airplane when you have the correct amount of money or Lease with the Option to Buy.

996. It's a sad crazy mixed up world out there but you are the one who can ignore all the negative things that happen to you in any given day or that people say to you to stir the pot: you don't need a persons' negativity.

995. You have a right not to loan anybody one single dime, anything you won't get back right away or to talk somebody's ears off as maybe they don't want to hear it.

994. You have a right to an Attorney if you should commit a horrific crime or any crime that gets you into trouble: don't go looking for trouble because you feel like nobody loves you: why are you starting shit with people??? Answer that question: because you are miserable or somebody did something wrong to you because they think the world owes them a living.

993. You can listen to Healing Music all day and all night long to heal your precious body, mind, soul & spirit. If that's what you need to do to heal your precious body, mind & soul.

992. When somebody comes knocking at your door you can tell them to leave or you can invite them in by asking them if they want sex with you. You just never know when you're going to be attracted to somebody. Also, when it's a religious group trying to get you to convert to their faith just start taking your clothes off and they'll leave and never come back ever again.

991. You can choose to answer your door naked when you feel like it. You'll get your point across.

990. If you don't like the way you look, put on a ton of makeup. Makeup does wonders for the body, mind, soul & spirit!

989. When in doubt, do a cost benefit analysis? This means comparing the cost of two objects to each other and finding out which one is the better deal.

987. There's really nothing wrong with you. All those Negative Messages you received as a child are no longer Negative. They become self-fulfilling prophecies. STOP! hanging on to those negative words/phrases which bring you down: "I'm not good enough": when

will you be good enough?, "I am a worthless piece of sh*t." "Stop comparing your self to shit. You & shit don't belong in the same sentence. It was never really about you: it was about the parent or person who didn't accept themselves as they're still holding on to what their parents or that person said to them and it's a "self-fullfilling prophecy" that has NOTHING TO DO WITH YOU.

986. You can choose to share your money w/ people when you feel like it. As a matter of fact, going "Dutch" = you pay your own way all the time is the correct thing to do: that way you don't have to feel guilty about mooching off of people. Problem solved: you can't afford to go out with somebody then ask them if they can afford to pay your way and you can pay them back later or it's a freebie. Learn to ask for what you want with your life. Don't be a victim all your life: you don't need that.

985. Rose are red, violets are blue but most of all I love you! Make sure that you say it to people that you especially like and to yourself until it really DOES SINK IN!!!

984. Roses are red, violets are blue but most of all I like you! Another phrase you can say to somebody that you like.

983. The older you get the closer you get to death, but who doesn't get closer to death the older they get??? Be grateful that you can do anything when you are Older. There is no such thing as the word "old" in your vocabulary. It simply doesn't exist.

982. When buying a Used Vehicle there are two things to consider: Rust which never sleeps & the mileage on the odometer. Everything else is a piece of cake. Sometimes, it's best to save money for a down payment

for a new vehicle and to do a cost benefit analysis: do you really need a brand new vehicle or can you live with buying a "showroom" model at a steep discount???!!!

981. The older you become the wiser you will become as you will learn to let go of all the bullsh*t you've let people put you through thru the years because you couldn't say "NO" and you were afraid to "speak up for yourself: it's called being "assertive". A great book to read about being assertive is called Getting To YES: Negotiating Agreement Without Giving In – Roger Fisher and William Ury Of the Harvard Negotiation Project. Penguin Books Ltd. Buy a copy of it used or brand new thru your nearest bookseller or online or get a FREE .PDF of it when you can find it online.

980. When in doubt, sus it out: Figure it out: you can do anything that you set your heart energy to, not necessarily your mind.

979. There is more to life than making money all of the time. There really is. Just make sure that you develop ETHICS about the making of the money or you will develop a reputation with being a dishonest person and you simply do not want that.

978. There is such a thing as a FREE LUNCH, DINNER or BREAKFAST or BRUNCH. Anyone who says there isn't is lying to you!!! Don't believe their hype.

977. The best time of the day or night to do anything is RIGHT NOW...Git 'Er Done!

976. You can choose to rent a hot air balloon by the session.

975. When shopping for food it's better to go on a full stomach as then you will not be tempted to buy as much if any food as your stomach is full. That' how it works: that's also a great way to try to lose weight: if you really don't like being FAT then you'd better start counting calories and measure portions when you're not busy being sick.

974. The word Depreciation sucks. It really does. As soon as you drive a brand new car off the lot it's worth half of what it was worth on the lot: what's up with that???!!!

973. Its ok to try to make people laugh w/ truly tasteless jokes. A lot of people think they are comedians but they don't practice their craft. It's best to practice your craft in front of the mirror. Memorize a hundred jokes and you'll thank me much later: if you're going to become great at anything you have to make sure that you PRACTICE, PRACTICE, PRACTICE ALL THE TIME until you develop the self-confidence to get what you're saying correct: that's how life works: the rest will take care of itself.

972. Its ok to keep a diary to write about what you accom- plished during the day and what went wrong and how to make things better the next time and to stop making mistakes.

971. When somebody insults you, don't respond. Just walk away! Or, start laughing until you are done with what they're saying and then walk away.

970. When somebody tells you to go to hell tell them, "I've already been there. t's nice anytime of the year but especially during the winter. And, I love talking to the Devil. You are the Devil right???"

969. You can choose not to use any punctuation in your sen- tences when you want to: it will drive Grammar Queens absolutely nuts just plain nuts.

968. When it's raining outside be glad that Mother Nature loves you. Even if it is windy & stormy. You can always choose to go for a walk and get all wet and makes sure that if it's thunder & lightening that you can walk in the open spaces, not the trees as the lightening when it does strike will strike an object like a tree, a house or anything with electricity in it before it strikes you.

965. The Illuminati & Nerubians who identify themselves as 'The Enlightened Ones' are truly a miserable bunch of misa- ligned people. They're not Enlightened. They're greedy and more and want to control, manipulate and dominate the world and your reality.

964. You have been here before. Why sweat the small stuff??? What are your "life lessons": write them down on a pad of paper and learn them: this is what you came here to learn. Learn those lessons. Keep them close to your heart.

963. You can eat cake and ice cream when you feel like it. Whoever says that you cannot is lying to you. Don't believe everything that you hear: learn to tune things and people out: buy yourself a set of ear plugs if you must.

962. Is it ok to drink yourself to death??? This only means that you have a "Sugar Imbalance" and that you're not capable of overcoming your "Emotional Pain Body" and that you failed miserably: You might also have a major case of low self-esteem. In order to stop "enabling the emotional pain body" you're going to have to sit down and write out

what keeps you in pain and why your EGO keeps doing this to you: do you really want to be in pain for the rest of your life or do you want to be FREE??? See point #   .

961. The Sun Always Shines On T.V. – A-Ha

960. When writing a book of any kind make sure that you get the research done as you are writing the book. And, make sure that you give proper credit to all of the people who helped you to write the book.

959. When it snows, be glad that it snows. Snow has a particular vibration all unto itself. So does everything else. You're going to have to learn that not everybody likes your V I B R A T I O N S: you're not here to become an "ass kisser": you'll only end up making people happy and you'll be the last person in the room to make yourself HAPPY!!! You don't want that.

958. When you have to move to a different land, be glad that you can do anything when you get there. Just make sure that your papers are all in order and that you renew your Green Card in the country that you are in. You don't want to go to jail for not doing so when you get into trouble for any reason and you get "greenlighted" or "gaslighted".

957. You can always become a Disability Queen and learn to live with no money in your pockets and not be able to pay your bills like a responsible adult!!!
956. You have the right to remain silent unless asked questions by a person of Authority or until your lawyer is present to represent you in a court of law, etc. Just make sure that you don't say anything that

incriminates you as then you're going to have to pay and fine and possibly go to jail. You don't want that.

955. Most people are wolves in sheep's clothing. They really are. Don't buy into their programs. You don't need the bullshit. Also, make sure that you don't end up becoming Gullible and end up writing a book called "Gullibles Travels" as you really don't want that.

954. All the bills you are not able to pay in this lifetime will be paid in the next lifetime. It's called Kharma & Dharma: do your best to pay off your debt file in this lifetime before you die. And, don't worry about or obsess over your bills: make sure that you pay the bills that you need to pay regularly so that you don't end up homeless & in the streets. You also don't want that either.

953. This is a really long book so I'm going to take a break right now. Breaks are good to take no matter what you do with your life. They really are.

952. Now that I've had my Cup 'o Tea break I feel refreshed.

951. A sense of humor is **REQUIRED** to get thru your life.

950. Make sure that you laugh your butt off 50++ times per day to get those endorphins going and the serotonin re-uptake inhibitors firing on all pistons. I highly recommend doing THAT! Laugh about anything and nothing: that's why I'm **HERENOW**!!!

949. The early bird gets the worm. He or she really does.

948. If the early bird doesn't get the worm then the early bird can always choose to eat something else. That's how birds operate: they don't always eat worms. They do eat other things like

947. 'Tis better to see **THE Sunny Side of Your Life**. You really have no other choice and being miserable and letting your EGOIC MIND screw you through life isn't the way to go or be.

946. When it's dark outside is it really so dark that you think a whole day has passed you by or that it really is dark outside. I dislike it when that happens. It really screws with the mind.

945. I am a teacher. All human beings are teachers whether we like to admit it or not.

944. A Syllabus is an Outline of the coursework that will be accomplished during the school semester of whatever it is that you choose to study w/ a teacher and their students.

943. When in doubt, get just the facts straight and nothing else: this is all you can really do with your fun & funny life: make life a fun thing to do all the time. No sense in being miserable all of the time: what does that get sweet, wonderful, likeable you???

942. You can choose to listen to any kind of music you like at any hour of the day or night. You can choose to listen to music 24/7 when you like. You'll know when it is time to quit listening to the music and get back to doing what needs to be done.

941. Drink alcohol when you want to. Be reasonable in your intake of alcohol. After all, life is all about having fun fun fun no matter how you feel when you start doing what you do

940. You can choose to smoke cigarettes while you are drinking alcohol. This only means that you are hyper. Same goes for any other addictions that you've got going: this is your "emotional pain body" reaching out

for healing or you just like your addictions: don't let them get in the way of living your life to your fullest.

939. You can choose to smoke a big phat joint to calm down when you like. Just so you can feel what love feels like as you're getting baked or once you do get baked. The next time that you are not "feeling the love" with yourself then think about the last time you got baked and how that made you feel.

938. The older you get the more medical issues you are going to have. Trust me on that one. I'm older and wiser but not dead yet!!! Take "nutritional supplements" if you must but never overdo them: vitamins should only be taken 2-3 times per week as they build up in your system and you end up wasting money from overdoing them.

937. When you are young you don't seem to have a care in the world. You live to play and play to live. So what if you don't have friends. You are your own best friend. You can live without friends as, "friends won't be around, friends will let you down, all you need are friends???" Jody Whatley sang about that situation. Sometimes, a friendship cannot last as you can't like each other enough to keep being friends: don't keep attracting to the wrong people with your life.

936. When life throws lemons at you make lemonade.

935. You may be the source of your own grief but what would life be like without the ability to grieve??? You would explode all over the place and somebody would actually have to clean up that mess.

934. You can make your own music. You really can.

933. You can work w/ other people to help you make your own music. You really need to unless of course, you are musical genius: then you're all set there aren't you???

932. The Sun has been here for millions of years. It's not going anywhere anytime soon. And, contrary to belief and opinion the Sun isn't going incinerate the Earth anytime soon.

931. You Are A Beautiful Person!

930. Having a job is a great thing as it keeps money rolling in and helps to keep you happy. Don't sabotage your jobs that you get: if you do then you're going to have to ask the question: "why do I keep doing this to myself???" Are you really that miserable or do you really not like that job??? Make sure that you get the training that you need to keep the job and not lose it because you didn't get the proper training you needed to know how to do the job. That's very important.

929. Having an extended family is nice.

928. Being close to anyone is a miracle.

927. You can get emotional love & care from just about anyone.

926. When you get arrested you go to jail and you have 3 square meals a day. Do you really want to keep doing that??? It gets very expensive at some point and you learn not to do that anymore. Some people keep getting themselves arrested as they like going to jail and not paying their ticket.

925. Anyone in a position of **Authority** can be ignored. You don't have to push their buttons.

924. When you get sick, there is a turning point at which you start to get better and heal. If you keep getting sick then what's the lesson here???!!! Learn your lessons and don't keep getting sick. You don't need that.

923. You can choose to use chemicals or Organic Healing to heal.

922. When there is doubt that just means you are not sure of yourself. You can ask yourself why that is and answer the question honestly.

921. It's nice to own things but the things that you own do not define you or own you unless you let them own you and define you. You own and define who you are and what you do.

920. When you cannot make a decision this only means that you will make the decision some other time. If you never make the decision only you & your maker will know about it and anybody else who is involved in the making of that decision.

919. It's really great to create **WIN/WIN Situation**s with your life.

918. You can go around being a Victim or a Victor. I choose being a Victor!!! I am VICTORIOUS IN EVERYTHNG THAT I DO!!!

917. The moon has a dark side & a light side. The Dark Side of The Moon is a classic pop/rock record by the group Pink Floyd.

916. Water is how some of us get to the other side.

915. "There is no such thing as death." **–Elizabeth Kubler Ross**

914. Everything is attached to Kharma & Dharma: Like it or not!!! So be very careful with your life and who you hang out with and what you say to those people, especially to people you live with and around. You

don't need their "negative vibrations" coming back at you through more verbal abuse.

913. When you think morose (very serious, unhappy & quiet) thoughts all the time you end up becoming them and you get very sick: why keep doing THAT???!!! You don't need those thoughts making you sick.

912. Sometimes it's great to get out of the house. But, only if you want to: but, don't let depression rule your life: there's already enough of that going around.

911. Sometimes it's good to sleep in. Most of the time it is not as when you do it will make your body feel very heavy and you might not want that.

910. Sometimes: well, sometimes is not an answer.

909. Being direct w/ people is the best way to be.

908. Living an honest life is the best way to go. You don't want a reputation for being a dishonest person and a prick or a cunt.

907. Give thanks for every day that you live another day.

906. Watching the sun rise in the morning is a beautiful thing.

905. Watching the sun set in the evening is also a beautiful thing.

904. **99.99%** of what you think never comes to pass: Be grateful for that.

903. A computer is only as good as the person who is using it. Sometimes, it's best to take a class in computers at the local job service or University. You'll learn more than you thought you'd learn on your own.

902. Being able to appreciate every moment is what counts.

901. Being able to get **Emotional Intimacy** from anyone is a wonderful thing. Some men and woman are not capable of that as they're too busy with their relationships with drugs and alcohol: time to move on with that person and not give in to their demands. They'll find somebody else to help them be an addict.

900. Being mad doesn't do you any good. Why are you mad at yourself, other people and the world: better keep a diary to answer those questions as life is much too short to be miserable all the time.

899. Getting even w/ someone who did you wrong doesn't even the score? It just means that you got even w/ the **S.O.B.** The next time you think about that person you will be right back to square one with them and wanting to get even with them: when is enough enough???

898. You can be as pissed off as anyone on the planet might get but it's really not going to do you any good. You can choose to rectify the situation by choosing to not be pissed off about it, be careful about your business doings and not get even with the person who did you wrong; It's all about them anyways, not you so why let them keep taking advantage of sweet, wonderful you: it just doesn't make any sense to keep letting somebody take advantage of you just because you like or are in love with them: Makes NO SENSE at all: do yourself a favor and get away from that behavior.

897. Being proactive about getting things done is the correct attitude. Slowly but surely you will achieve what you need to achieve with your life.

896. Being able to get rid of acne is a wonderful thing. There are many different solutions and you have to keep trying until you find the correct solution to your problem: sometimes, the 1st thing you try won't work. Keep trying until you get rid of your acne. Here are a ton of solutions to help get rid of acne: tea tree oil diluted, cinnamon oil, rose oil or rose water, lavender oil, clove oil, rosemary oil, lemongrass, basil, green tea, aloe vera, a zinc supplement, brewers yeast, a fish oil supplement, honey cinnamon mask, limit dairy intake, reduce stress, apple cider vinegar, witch hazel

895. Life doesn't always work out the way you want it to work out. Sometimes, you just can't push a square into a round hole no matter how hard you keep trying or how long: try a different approach.

894. When somebody asks you if you'd like to go on a date w/ them ask them if there are any strings attached and where they 're going to take you. It's on them, not you: you can always choose to say, "No, I'm not really interested." Worst comes to worse: you can always tell them that if they don't stop bugging you that you'll put a "Protection From Abuse" on their nasty ass: that'll make them stop what they're doing.

893. Ask somebody to do something w/ you even if you don't know them. They might just say, "YES!" Example: going to a movie, going shopping with you, going some place to eat.

892. Being able to breathe in/out is a marvel of being human.

891. Finishing up something that you started a long time ago is a wonderful thing to accomplish. Remember: this is what your life is really all about: make sure that you don't put too much on your plate to get done/accomplish as you don't want to be walking around feeling

tired and used all the time: learn to say, "NO, I'm really not interested in helping you with your problems." Not today!!!

890. Not finishing up something that you started only means you didn't think it thru before you started the project. You can finish up at a later date or abandon the project if you'd like to: nobody says that you have to keep putting yourself through hell.

889. Not every project you start gets finished: make sure that it's something that's realistic to be doing and that you'll get the help and proper guidance that you need in order to finish the project.

888. When somebody says mean things to you, you can choose to ignore them and look the other way. But, when that happens this only makes you want to vent to somebody so that you can get it out of your system: that's just the way humans are designed.

887. Eating healthy Organic Food is what life is really all about.

886. When you want something bad enough you will go out and get it and/or find a way to get it in your life: you can live without a car, a house, a job, etc. But, do you really want to??? Take a cold, hard, long look at what you really want in your life.

885. Not everything is meant to be. You are NOT GOD, GODDESS, or GODHEAD: you may think you are but you're really not: but, it's o.k. to think of yourself as being Godlike, Goddess like or Godhead like as we were all made by "Creator Gods," so in essence we are related to God, Goddess, Godhead: God is everywhere.

884. There roughly 145 Careers that one can choose from. This is just something that I happen to know about from all of the Spiritual/Healing books I've read over the years.

883. The reason you are here is because you want to be here. You decided to be born all those years ago: just deal with it as best as you can: there's really no reason to keep being miserable your whole life: learn the lessons that you need to learn and be glad that you are HUMAN!!!

882. The reason you have a father and a mother is because you cannot have one without the other unless of course, you are a test tube baby. You'd still have a mother and a father and you'd just have been conceived in a test tube thru "invitro fertilization": then you would have been put into the mother's uterus to be grown and then delivered after 9 months. That's a very different story: Radical Science that came to pass in. Basically, in a nut shell: the manipulation of the egg and sperm for fertilization.

881. The only way to heal your self is to let go of your past or write about it to get it out of your system. At the very least you will have a book that you can publish and make some money off of with a real publisher or a self-publisher like Lulu, Amazon or ??? And, just because you wrote about your past doesn't mean that you've overcome it: you've just written a book that people can read that may help them to heal depending on what your message of HOPE & HEALING is.

880. When somebody tells you what you want to hear it may not be the best course of action to take. Don't believe everything that you hear as that's no way to live your life: some people are just "pathological liars".

They'll never stop lying as they don't know better and never will learn until somebody puts them in their place.

879. It's best to keep your mouth shut and ignore what goes on around you. You'll have a much better existence. Trust me on that one: minding your own business is the best thing that you can do as you know how human beings really are: they like to stir the pot and unfortunately you're their next victim: you don't need their b.s. Ignore them: you don't need more bullshit in your life.

876. Talking trash about people isn't the best course of action. If you keep having it out with somebody you can keep having it out with them or just tell them why you want them to stop doing what they're doing to you and what the consequences will be or just stop talking to that person altogether and when you see them don't say anything else to them: you don't need their hate and vitriol.

875. When it rains, sometimes it pours. But, it never rains cats and dogs: be thankful for THAT!!!

874. Everything in the World and the Universe has a vibration unique to itself. So do you: what kind of a Vibration or Tone do you want to put out to the world? That's what attracts people to you.

873. Just because someone is walking down the street and talking to themselves doesn't mean they are crazy. Maybe they need to vent or they're talking to themselves because they need to sort things out in their head.

874. When you hear somebody speaking to you they might actually be on a cell phone or any other device that has nothing to do with you.

873. Love Is The Healer: use it to heal yourself & the people in your Inner Circle.

872. Listening to the wind is a great exercise in and of itself.

871. People Need People. Be glad you have any friends.

870. A mouse can be an animal that comes from a field or that is attached to your computer.

869. Just because somebody looks at you the wrong way does n't mean that they are cross-eyed. Maybe they looked at you as they are not judging you. No big deal.

865. Mistaken Identity is a big deal. It can get you killed. Thank God that doesn't happen 99.99% of the time.

864. Being thankful for being Alive is the best thing you can do at any hour of the day or nite. The storms in your head will soon pass.

863. Meditation is a great thing to do in the morning & at nite.

862. If your forehead is flush maybe you just ate too much sugar or carbohydrates.

861. If you come from a Dysfunction Junction Family it's really no big deal. 85% of people choose to come from horrid conditions. It's how some of us learn to let go & learn our lessons. What are your life lessons.

860. Going to a University, Trade School or any Institution of Higher Learning is not necessarily the best course of action. Sometimes getting a job and seeing the Psychotherapist is the best option. You can go back to school when the time is right but never let anybody force you into

college, etc. There's plenty of time for that once you've thought it through.

859. There's nothing wrong with being GAY. This only means that you are HAPPY!!!

858. Being a lesbian only means that you don't relate to other men sexually speaking. That's not your problem: embrace your Sexuality.

857. If you knew how many different kinds of Sexuality there really are it would blow your mind. It's not just Heterosexuality and Homosexuality.

856. A flower is a beautiful thing to admire.

855. All flowers have healing capabilities.

854. Some flowers are so nasty you'd think that somebody cut the cheese.

853. Going for a drive on a Sunday afternoon in your vehicle or somebody else's vehicle is a blessed thing.

852. Climbing a mountain is a very fun thing to do.

851. Heal yourself and help others to heal.

850. Doing the wrong thing is never the best course of action. You have to live with what you did. Choose wisely.

849. When it gets really cold outside be thankful that you have a roof over your head. Some people don't have that and are starving to death. It's good to accept yourself in the Present Moments.

848. When it gets really hot outside be glad you can drink water.

847. The most precious commodity on the planet is water.

846. Those people who have a need to work within the Petro- leum Industry have a need to work within the Petroleum Industry.

845. Bells tell us many different things about ourselves.

844. Going to hell in a handbasket is not necessarily such a good thing.

843. Being able to work on your issues is a Blessing.

842. Choosing a Career that makes you a lot of money is a great thing.

841. Being able to steer your own ship is a wonderful thing.

840. Shadows & Light is what it is all about.

839. Being able to learn anything is really the best thing for anyone.

838. Being Indestructible is The Best!

837. If somebody didn't love you the way you wanted to be loved while growing up then it's never too late to love your self the way you need to be loved. Maybe the love you did get from your parent, etc. was the best that could be done!!!

836. Loose Lips Sink Big Ships. Really loose lips sink even bigger ships. Be careful whose ship you try to sink: it could come back on you.

835. Christmas is the time of the year to celebrate the coming of Christ. It's also a time to buy yourself a Christmas Present.

834. New Year's Day is the time of the year when we celebrate going out w/ a bang!

833. If you really want to lose weight, walk around in the cold practically naked all the time. Lose the weight by freezing yourself.

832. Anyone who is obsessed w/ losing weight might have a body image problem. They might also have low self-esteem. It could also be caused by Society telling US we need to look good all the time, etc.

831. When somebody is yelling at you are they really yelling at you. Maybe what they tell you is what they are telling themselves. Ignore them?

830. Green & Brown are colors for people who like being stable. Maybe you should wear green or brown or both colors. What's your favorite color: wear that.

829. The Center of Light in Your World is located in your spine.

828. When you need to go within all you have to do is breathe or imagine yourself being healed on the spot from within.

827. Tibetan Bells are a great way to loosen up, relax & chill out.

826. Owning any musical instrument is a blessing. Learn how to play it when you want to.

825. It's never too late to have a happy childhood.

824. Being able to speak to anyone on the telephone is a great thing. Imagine how far we've come thanks to Alexander Graham Bell.

823. Sometimes you have to perform 1000's of experiments to get something just right. Sometimes it's a 100. Sometimes the answer is right underneath your nose.

822. 'Tis a great thing to be able to cut the cheese.

821. A friend in need is a friend indeed.

820. Be Thankful. Step aside from your busy life and just be Thankful.

819. You Are An Amazing Person.

818. If somebody wants you to hate them openly ask them why. You can choose to ignore them.

817. Who are your favorite recording artists in the world? These are the people who Inspire you to be yourself.

816. Being able to go out to eat at a restaurant is a wonderful thing. Especially when it is Organic.

815. Sometimes all you have to do is open up a window to circulate air and feel a breath of fresh air.

814. Being able to ride your mountain bike up and down the street is a lot of fun.

813. Being able to fix something that requires a great deal of precision is such a gas but a great gas nevertheless.

812. When you want to really know how to fix things, fix them yourself. Pay attention or use your cell phone to record the steps it took to fix something and make it run again.

811. Flying halfway around the world on a leer jet is Fun Fun Fun.

812. Motion Sickness is your body's way of telling you that you and water don't get along, etc.

810. Sometimes you don't need a reason to be thankful. You just are!

809. Eating Ice Cream is such a great way to ruin your teeth. It's best done infrequently.

808. When someone wants your attention they'll get your attention. Be careful who it is. Screen people out regularly to keep certain people out of your life: you don't need their b.s.

807. When you are getting tired this means you might get cranky and need a break just like children do.

806. Reading a book and walking at the same time is asking for trouble. It's like talking on the cell phone or .txtng while walking. You might have an accident.

805. Sometimes the phone rings when you are sleeping. You can choose not to answer it or you can do yourself a favor and turn it completely off at nite so you can get some much needed sleep.

804. A pet is a wonderful thing to have and take care of. Pets are like children. They deserve love and attention, not hell.

803. When somebody tells you to go to hell just smile back at them and say, "I'm already there. I'm speaking to the Devil!"

802. Getting away with murder is not such a good thing.

801. Double Jeopardy is not such a bad place to be if you don't mind it.

800. I am happy to be alive.

799. Sometimes it's impossible to pay all of your bills all at once. Do the bills gradually. Use the 'envelope system' if you must.

798. When most of us die we have a Debt Load that is so high that that is what we have. It's going to affect our next life as it has to be paid off karmically speaking.

797. Don't listen to anyone unless its life or death. Take every- body else w/ a grain of salt.

796. The hardest thing you will ever do is Love Your Self! Instead of it being hard make it easy to love yourself.

795. Just Do It!

794. Being able to visualize happiness is the best feeling in the world.

793. Having a good ear for listening to other people is a great thing.

792. A ledger is a great empty book to own.

791. There is a difference between eating foods grown and processed w/ chemicals vs foods that are made w/ pure love that are Organically Grown.

790. It's such a wonderful feeling to know that people actually care about YOU!

789. When somebody hurts you they are only hurting them- selves. Pain is a human emotion. Without pain what would we know???

788. We have 6 senses.

787. Having a comfortable pair of walking shoes is a great thing.

786. Being able to pay your bills on time is a great thing. When you can't, you can't. Don't fret the small stuff.

785. Money has a Vibration all its own. Most people don't know how to think & feel about having money in their lives. Analyze how much money is enough: write on your checks and correspondence: BLESSINGS or a word that helps you to be thankful for being able to pay your bills.

784. A position of lack means that you may not be trying hard enough or too focused on what you really want. Give up your thoughts to God/The Universe and maybe it will come back to you.

783. When it snows, it snows. Snow is like Sex. You never know how many inches you'll get or how long it will last.

782. Being able to do anything correctly is priceless. If at 1st you don't succeed then try again until you get it right.

781. Being lazy is not such a good thing. Try becoming more productive. You'll notice the difference.

780. Having a lot of money in your life isn't the be all end all. When you have a lot of money in your life you have to manage it correctly or find somebody who doesn't mind managing it for you and who won't rip you off.

779. You can get high anytime you like. It's called living your life.

778. FREEDOM is such a precious thing. Cherish it!!!

777. Being stuck inside something might not be such a good thing. Unless of course, this is what you like and it gets your blood moving.

776. If there is a gap between your teeth why bother fixing it?

775. As soon as a relationship becomes verbally or physically abusive you can choose to leave. You can also choose to get help. You don't have to keep putting up with anybody's crap for a long time.

774. Sulphur is one of those things that some people don't mind sniffing. I love it.

773. The older I get the more I have to pay attention to my body and correct eating.

772. The thing I want is the thing I want. I will get it one way or the other. If I don't get it then I don't get it. There will be other chances on down the road and is it meant to be???

771. If something is out of your reach, get a step-stool, step- ladder, a ladder to reach it or a grabber.

770. The older one becomes, the harder it is to get anything done.

769. Oh to be in love again and never get out of it…

768. Being able to sit around in your domicile N A K E D is a blessing.

767. Being able to count forward and backward is something to do.

766. Everybody is a genius at something. Trust me on that one. Even Con-Artists.

765. Being able to say, "NO!" or "YES!" is a blessing.

764. We live in the Milky Way Galaxy. There are other Galaxies out there.

763. Selling a million copies of anything really is something.

762. Selling nothing at all means you're probably selling people 'False Hope'.

761. Eating a candy bar is a lot of fun.

760. When your cat brings you dead things the cat is trying to show you affection. The cat might also be trying to tell you what an asshole you really are!

759. You don't always have to speak to get your point across.

758. You can choose to be a meat eater.

756. You can choose to be a Vegetarian.

755. You can choose to be a meat eater & a Vegetarian.

754. The sky is great when it's blue.

753. The sky is crying when it is grey but that's ok. It's still going to be a Beautiful Day.

752. You can love everybody.

751. You can choose to love no one.

750. Losing weight is a great thing to do.

749. Gaining all the weight you lost back is an even greater thing to do. All that means is Start Over!

748. Don't listen to everything that Society tells you to do. Some things that Society says are correct are totally incorrect. Ex. It's not ok to discriminate against Gay People as how would you feel if they did this to you? You wouldn't like it. So, don't do it.

747. Break Out of Your Self-Imposed Shell

746. When you are depressed this is your body's way of telling you that you are not doing enough to take care of yourself. Just cut out the pity party and when you cannot do that then you can just keep yourself busy and that will make you happier & take your mind off of being depressed. Depression is basically not doing enough.

745. Getting older is a wonderful thing. Growing older grace- fully is priceless.

744. You can choose to learn anything you want most anytime you like and practically anywhere you like.

743. When its grey outside this only means that the old man is snoring.

742. When its blue outside this only means that the old man is awake and having a great time.

741. Its ok to be yourself no matter what the outcome.

740. Its ok to love somebody even when they don't love you back. Maybe they're thinking about you but not showing you physically. That's a part of being human.

749. Having a car to get around with and in is a great thing.

748. Having any mode of transportation is a great thing.

747. Taking a jet plane anywhere is a great thing to do. Coming back to where you live is priceless.

746. Its ok not to love anyone.

745. A relationship isn't the true benchmark of happiness. Lov- ing your self is.

744. When in doubt you can figure most anything out.

743. The time between being awake and twilight is an amazing time to be Alive.

742. Its ok to make a decision about doing something and then changing your mind at the last minute not to do it. Nobody says you have to do anything: that decision is all on you.

741. When life throws lemons at you make lemonade.

742. It does not good to hold on to old feelings of anger, animosity, hate & wanting to get even. Let them go.

741. When someone or somebody screws you over be grateful that it's not happening over and over and over again. When you decide to get even w/ that person or group of people don't tell anyone what you did when confronted: don't say anything.

740. When you feel all emotional it's ok to cry. Big Boys do cry. So do Big Girls.

739. Eating a peach is really fun to do.

738. If your parents didn't love you while you were growing up it's not your fault. It's really no one's fault. It's never too late to start loving yourself and treating yourself w/ the respect that you never got from them or anyone else. They did the best that they could: that's all that you can expect. Nothing else.

737. 90% of a case is having Physical Evidence. 10% is circumstantial. If you 're going to commit a crime think of 25 reasons you might get caught. Is committing the crime worth getting caught???

736. When it snows outside its 32 degrees out or colder.

735. Putting up a Christmas tree once a year is a great thing to do to celebrate the birth of Christ and being Christian, Catholic or whatever religion you are a believer in. You can also leave the tree up all year long if you like.

734. Taking the Christmas tree down is priceless. Especially when it's a natural tree. Have fun cleaning the pine cones and the needles off the floor if it's real.

733. When you go shopping and you get home from shopping and you have to tinkle, you'll have no problem w/ opening the door w/ a key and rushing to the bathroom. So what if you don't make it in time.

732. After you go to the bathroom you are always relieved.

731. There's no place like home, There's no place like home. There's no place like home, There's no place like home.

730. In order to become a peace loving person you must think peaceful loving thoughts.

729. You have to go through a lot of people to get the answers you are looking for w/ your life. Don't always expect answers. You might not get them. Work on Solutions to your problems.

728. Having a steak as your dinner is priceless.

727. You can eat a bean curd turkey for Thanksgiving if you don't want to eat a Turkey and all of the fixins.

726. When the temperature is just right that means that you will feel better.

725. Having a computer to type these words into is a wonderful thing.

724. When a person is mean to you they are only expressing the way they feel. It's best not to let them get the best of you. You can question that person but do it in a way that is gentle and that teaches the person to not do it again.

723. Its ok to pick up a new habit even if that means you've been putting it off for 40 years. It's never too late to start anything even if that means it's a do over!

722. Coming up w/ 1001 Reasons to Be Thankful isn't the hardest thing in the world.

721. Getting to No. 1 is going to be a great reason to publish this book with an actual publisher.

720. Somebody already wrote a book about this so why am I doing it? Because I want to and I can.

719. When you run out of energy to get things done then take a break and recoup your energy and finish what you started.

718. When you don't make it to the bathroom you can clean up the mess you made.

717. When the Fall arrives and the leaves start falling off of the trees after they have turned red, golden orange & brown that is such a wonderful sight to see.

716. Be Grateful when you remember to be grateful.

715. When you cannot be grateful for being a live this is the time to reflect about all the good things that have happened in your lifetime. There must be something good that happened to you along the way. Ignore the bad things that happened as they're not happening anymore.

714. When your computer crashes it's fun to learn about why you need an anti-virus and a malware program in there to keep out unwanted viruses and threats to your computer. Be grate ful there's somebody to fix it for you FREE usually.

713. When you keep talking or writing about the same thing over and over and over again and you refuse to let something go that needs to be let go then you have to seriously question why it is that you refuse to let it go and what your Egoic Mind is trying to tell you. Abandon the Egoic Mind. It will only trick you into feeling bad about your self again.

712. When someone or a group of people refuses to do something with you you have to question your motives and their motives. Is it really worth it: find somebody else to help you accomplish what you want to do.

711. It's that small group of people who can and will always make a difference.

710. It's also that small group of people who can and will rip you off who don't make a difference: Banish them from your life permanently as they only care about one thing: Being truly indifferent to your feelings and ripping you off.

709. When you lose something this only means that you need to pay more attention next time.

708. Not paying your bills is a beatch.

707. When you are mean to somebody you have to question what brought that out of you and why you decided to be a mean person in the 1st place. Don't think too hard about what you decided to get even with that person. It's just something that you did. Forgive it. Otherwise, it will eat you up from the inside and show on the outside.

706. Having a great pair of walking shoes is a great thing so you can go walking, running or hiking anywhere you like.

705. Be grateful for injuries. The injuries are only telling you to pay more careful attention to not have an accident.

704. Taking responsibility for your actions is PRICELESS!

703. Getting a job is a great thing. If you can hold on to it is even better.

702. Flying under the radar is only going to work when you act like you know what you are doing and you deal with the fear of being caught. Be thorough.

701. The world is full of treachery, lechery and deceit. The only way to deal with that is to not get caught in a trap.

700. I made it to No. 700. Hooray! Hooray!

699. It's time to take a break. A break from anything is a good thing. Actually, it's great. Above all else, make sure that you pace yourself and that you never let anyone rush you through life. This only means that you're doing your job correctly even when you do make mistakes. Mistakes show you what you're doing wrong!!!

698. 'Tis a great thing to be able to drink boiled water and not that crap that comes out of the tap.

697. 'Tis an even better thing to be able to drink filtered water.

696. It's ok to go around feeling all dejected but who is it hurting???

695. Listening to Pop Music or any kind of music is a wonderful thing to do at any time of the day or night.

694. When it's time to do something else, go do it. Have fun w/ whatever you do.

693. When you fall in love with someone run like hell if the person doesn't want to love you back. This only means that you've fallen in love w/ the wrong person. Maybe they are incapable of 'Emotional Intimacy'. That's not your problem. It's their problem, not yours.

692. It's always best to be on the same page w/ everyone you work with.

691. The turnaround point is not when you give up. It's when you keep pushing onward and actually succeed. Never give up. That's the lesson.

690. It's ok to be addicted to anything. Just don't overdo it.

689. If the only way you can stay sane is to go to AA Meetings then go to them. People can be such a wonderful help to you.

688. Its ok not to have any money in your pockets. There will be more down the line.

687. Its ok to have a lot of money in your pockets. But, make sure that if it's cash not to be traveling on an Amtrack train as the government has "search & seizure laws" that shouldn't even be. Nobody has a right to seize your money and assume that it's drug money.

686. Technically I'm supposed to carry $1,000.00 of spending money in my pockets just in case something bad happens. You never know when you're going to need to bail yourself out of jail for something that you did.

685. I don't carry $1,000.00 in my pockets ever so if you think you're going to rip me off it's never going to happen. I simply won't allow it. Been there, done that. I don't have time for con artists anymore. Neither should you.

684. If your clothes are too tight, lose some weight by eating only half of what you put on your plate.

683. You can always buy bigger clothes to fit into but why bother with that. You are only going to end up filling them up with more weight so instead of doing that explore the Option of why you are gaining weight in the 1st place. Is it a glandular problem or your eyes are bigger than they really should be???

682. If at 1st you don't succeed, you can always try again until you don't succeed or you do succeed. If you fail miserably, I'm not going to tell you, "I told you so." There is already that critic or critics who will criticize you so I don't need to be playing that game with you or anyone else. Get it right the 1st time, that's the main thing.

681. When you do a belly flop in the water make sure you don't do it when you are spread eagle with the water just before im- pact.

680. If you must cry, then do so in front of people so that they can ask why you are upset. It's ok to cry in front of people even if that means you are going to be embarrassed! I do it all the time. It has nothing to do with the fact that I'm weak or not: I'm just processing intense emotions.

679. Whats Love Go To Do With It: what's love but a 2nd hand emotion. Do you really want that when it doesn't work out???

678. You can't be too successful.

677. Its ok to fail your way through life and then finally succeed at what you are good at. Failing your way into becoming a successful person is what it is all about: just don't take it too personally when things don't work out: you'll eventually hit your stride.

676. When the time is right you will bloom like a flower.

675. The Sun may shine after a storm. So what if it doesn't: eventually the Sun will start shining again.

674. If it wasn't for storms in life, we'd all be crazy.

673. Its ok to make the disconnect from your family for the rest of your life if they don't accept you for who you are and who you've become because they can't deal with their own past.

672. Its ok to meditate during the middle of the day.

671. It's never too late to accept yourself with all of your faults. There must be something good about you. Sometimes you have to overlook the bad to get to the good in you. Everybody has something to say.

670. The word good is a qualifier for a description of an object, not a person but frequently the word is used to describe your state of mind. It's simply not true. Well describes your state of mine, good describes an object.

669. The word bad is a qualifier for a description of an object, not a person but frequently the word is used to describe your state of mind. It's simply not true. Well describes your state of mind, bad describes an object.

668. Snow has a vibration all its own.

667. Learn to appreciate snow even though it may be very cold outside.

666. Shoveling snow may not be good for your back but that's ok. It's exercise.

665. When in doubt, work it out.

664. When you are tired and sleepy, this only means that you either didn't get enough sleep, there may be something wrong with you and the medications you are talking or there is a phys- ical problem with your body that needs to be addressed.

663. There is nothing wrong with you. There never was. Just because someone didn't want to get emotionally close to you as a child doesn't mean that you are a bad person. The person who didn't want to get close to you emotionally had major hang-ups. It's not your fault and had nothing to do with you.

662. Its ok to feel grumpy. Doesn't matter what your age is: we all get that way sometimes.

661. Its ok to feel any other emotion you want to feel. You are human. Relish that thought. There are 27 categories of emotions in a human being with subtleties from there on.

660. Going shopping at any time of the day or night is a great thing to do.

659. Listening to Ambient Sounds or Electronic Music is a great way to relax.

658. Earplugs can make the difference between being crazy and killing someone. Buy yourself a set of good quality ear plugs to block those ears to mask out noises around you so you can get some calm & peace in your life and sleep at night.

657. Some people will never have any respect for anyone as they operate totally on the level of fear.

656. When it's your time to go you will know.

655. If you feel that badly about yourself then you may as well go someplace where people are suffering and that will make you feel much better.

654. The problems of the world are not yours. They are the problems of the world. You don't need to become a martyr like Jesus did or anybody else for that matter.

653. A lot of people who were abused as children have to spend their Adult lives being angry, full of rage and generally unhappy. Be thankful

you are not being abused (verbally, emotionally, physically) anymore. You were a very strong person to survive that shit.

652. It's possible to have a good day.

651. It's possible to have a really bad day from hell.

650. Just because someone doesn't smile at you is no reason to get mad. That person has all they can do to survive in the present moment. Maybe they will smile later. Maybe they won't but don't take their response personally. It's not your fault and you can't make people do what they're not ready to do.

649. It's never too late to have a happy childhood.

648. Just because somebody told you, "You can't do that," doesn't mean that it can't be done. Do it if it makes you feel good.

647. Loose lips sink big ships. Really loose lips sink even bigger ships.

646. You have all you can do to be the person you are right now. Relish that thought.

645. It's never too late in the Season to go and ride a roller- coaster. Just make sure you know when the last day of the Season is so you don't end up missing out on a really good time by yourself or with your friends.

644. It's never too late in the Season to go to a water park and ride the water rides.

643. Just because someone is sexually attracted to you doesn't mean that you have to have sex with that person. If they won't stop bothering

you, tell them you have a sexually transmittable disease. That works every time.

642. Having fun in life no matter what is the goal.

641. When somebody calls you in the middle of the nite it's probably a pervert who wants sex, not a massage.

642. Crank calls are fun to make but does anyone benefit from them??? If they're funny and you get a great laugh out of it.

641. My life's mission is to have fun no matter what happens to me.

640. I like having fun as it makes me feel better.

639. Deciding that I am going to have a miserable day is only going to make me miserable. May as well decide to have a Fun Fun Fun Day.

638. If you don't like the scenery you can always change it by going someplace else or change the channel on your television.

637. If you don't like the restaurant you are eating at you can always go someplace else. Just make sure you haven't ordered your meal yet.

636. Apple Cider Vinegar is one of life's great healing elixirs. It's a tonic that is great for a myriad of problems like balancing out your PH in your body and making you regular, helping you to lose weight when done regularly and with healthy food.

635. Let 'em eat cake. Or make 'em a cake to eat and give it to 'em.

634. One of life's greatest treasures is being caught in the pre- sent moments.

632. You can always take a class in parachuting and make sure you learn how to pack your parachute perfectly every time. Otherwise, it might not turn out so well. Thoroughly check your work and make sure that it's done correctly.

631. Bungee jumping is a no no as frequently the person doing their job doesn't do it by forgetting to do something correctly and people end up hurt, dead or drowned. Life's too short to go bungee jumping.

630. Don't believe the hype. It's just hype.

629. Just because you are thankful doesn't mean that you're not going to have problems with your life. Problems only tell us to move on and to be grateful.

628. Hope is sometimes soap on a rope.

627. Just because somebody looks crazy doesn't mean they are crazy. Maybe there's a an actual soul in there who is nice, fri- endly and kind. You can't always judge a book by its cover.

626. Some of the craziest people in the world are the sanest people in the world.

625. Remember to smile as much as you can. It's good for releasing Endorphins and Serotonin in your brain.

624. You can always walk around with an upside down frown but then that would make you an upside down clown.

623. When somebody rips you off emotionally, physically, spiritually, etc. that's exactly what happened. You can choose to get even with

that person or you can never let it happen again by learning your lessons.

622. It's very good to eat healthy food that encourages di- gestion.

621. You can choose to eat any kind of food you like but will you enjoy it??? Eat what you like but make sure that you eat balanced foods.

620. Growing a garden is a very tough thing to do. But, it can be done.

619. Just because you were raised by Control Freaks doesn't mean that you cannot learn how to become one. Maybe they were just under Emotional Clods who were very dense Spiritual beings having a Human Experience.

618. Taking things personally all the time is no way to live. Lighten Up!!!

617. Sometimes, when a person doesn't want to love you back might mean that that person is emotionally incapable of taking care of their own emotional needs. It's best to forget about them. They will only end up breaking your heart. Move On!!!

616. If you don't like hearing birds chirping outside your win- dow, you can always put in earplugs and shut the windows.

615. Just because someone told you you can't do something doesn't mean that it can't be done.

614. Defy the expectations and the odds of succeeding.

613. You can do anything you set your mind to.

612. Just because you give up on finishing a project doesn't mean that it won't get finished down the road.

611. Life is a series of lessons. You win some, you lose some: make sure you come out on the winning side of things.

610. You have a right not to get into a relationship that is verbally or physically abusive or both. Nobody wins except the Abuser and you don't want to end up in the hospital or get killed from trying too hard to placate the son of a bitch or bastard. Move Away as soon as you can.

609. Life's is too short to miserable.

608. You can Meditate any time of the day or night. If you fall asleep, such is your life. You can always meditate again later and get better at doing it.

607. People have no right to make demands of you. Don't kow tow to their selfish needs: make them responsible for their own demands. Create WIN/WIN Situations.

606. Just because it's raining outside doesn't mean you can't go for a walk in the rain without a raincoat.

605. Umbrellas were designed to keep you from getting totally drenched. Investing in one is a good idea.

604. When it rains outside, that is the best time to sell umbrellas.

603. Becoming an alcoholic only means that you are addicted to sugar. You have a major sugar imbalance going on in your body.

602. Some people are simply not able to overcome their addic- tions. Be glad you can overcome your demons.

601. Marijuana is not a drug. It is an herb. Use it wisely. Don't abuse it.

600. Sometimes, you don't need a reason to be thankful.

559. Having a car is a luxury.

558. Owning a house is a luxury.

557. Learning how to say, "NO!" is a great thing. Keep saying it until you can say it without feeling guilty. If all else fails you can say, "Go love yourself," but most people take that as something else which it's really not.

556. Say, "YES!" only to things you absolutely, positively want. Don't say yes because you can't say no. Say, "I'll get back to you on that question." You are not required to say, "Yes!" just be- cause somebody is too lazy to do something by themselves or doesn't have the funds to do it. That's not your issue: it's theirs. Tell them to go to a bank or credit union to get a loan as they're being very lazy and asking for your help: it's not up to you to enable people. That's not your job.

555. It's not wise to take anybody's inventory unless you are ready for the emotional fallout. Sometimes it's better to step on your lips.

554. It's a beautiful world. Have fun with your life. It's not all about doom & gloom as the powers that be want you to think.

553. This book is so long I don't know if it will ever get finished. That's ok.

551. You can eat cake.

550. You can eat ice cream.

549. It's ok to eat the cake without the ice cream and vice versa.

548. When in doubt, figure it out.

547. White Paper is either paper you use for drawing or white paper on a computer screen.

546. Why is Buddha so fat? Shouldn't he be thing to emphasize his Spirituality???

545. Mother Theresa against having an opulent life and would make people strip things down to their essential being before making an appearance somewhere. Maybe people did that for her as they were honoring her charitable spirit but it ended up costing the hotel or business a lot of money to de-emphasize opulence.

544. Jesus was a martyr. You can choose to be a martyr but you will become a very miserable human being, wind up in jail or dead. That's your choice.

543. Do you think it really was true that Jesus was born through Mother Mary without Joseph making love to her???

542. There are going to be tyrants no matter where you live. It's best to ignore them. They mean nothing to you.

541. If it's very cold outside, you can always make a fire in the fireplace or turn on the heat.

540. Learn to listen to your body and what you can and cannot eat. You don't have any time to be sick from anything.

539. Sex is S-E-X. Sometimes you get it, most of the time you do not get it. That's ok.

538. The older you get the more you learn to do without.

537. Supposedly animals have sex only at different times of the year to carry on their offspring. Humans think about sex all the time, especially men. So do women, but, for different reasons.

536. The union between a man and a woman is not the only union possible. There are other types of unions out there.

535. Marriage is a scam and a sham. You don't have to buy into it if you don't want to.

534. When somebody tells you to go to hell agree with them and then ask them if they are the devil in disguise???

534. If someone tells you they just found God, give them plenty of room to move. They're going to have more problems on down the road.

533. Its ok to reject somebody outright.

532. If you don't like somebody's voice, it's ok to quit your job, but, make sure you let the employer know why you are quitting your job.

531. Every little mistake you make in life gets you closer to your goals.

530. Its ok to be angry and to hate everybody and the whole world. It happens to the best of us.

529. You can choose to go to self-help support groups or you can choose to not go to self-help support groups. Support groups won't necessarily solve your emotional & psychological problems.

528. When somebody makes demands of you you need to ask yourself if the demands are ok or if you don't want to acquiesce to that persons demands.

527. Its ok to have fun all the time.

526. When you are not having fun you have to ask yourself, "Why am I not having fun?" You will get an answer.

525. Fun should be everbody's middle name. We as human beings are here to have FUN FUN FUN!

524. The grass is always greener on the other side of the fence. Be glad for that thought.

523. Be glad you can tune people and the world out.

522. How many books do you want to write before you keel over??? That's totally up to you.

521. I've written 3 books so far. I'm working on 4 more.

520. Just because you think you are going to become successful at something doesn't mean that you can't become successful at something. Sometimes, you just have to keep studying to get there.

519. Its ok to drink boiled water. The water that comes out of your tap is poison in disguise.

518. Losing weight is a great thing to do but gaining it all back is even more fun. Or is it?

517. Just because you lost a lot of weight doesn't mean that you are an AIDS Patient.

516. There is more ignorance in the world than bliss.

515. Have a blissed out moment.

514. Nirvana is the happiest state you can reach.

513. When in doubt, make lemonade.

512. There is nothing wrong with being wrong.

511. Anytime you want to have sex w/ another human being is ok by me. Just make sure the person is in agreement w/ you.

510. Just because you can't get laid doesn't mean that you have to get upset.

509. Working on your issues is why you are here. Be grateful.

508. The air that we breathe is the most important thing in the world.

507. Falling off a ladder means you might not have been paying attention. Make sure that it never happens again as it will seriously impact your way of life.

506. There are only two fears a man has and a Social Anthropologist is going to tell you these two things: a fear of popping noises and a fear of heights. Believe It!

505. Not all other fears are imagined.

504. Imagining dragons is the stuff of myths. I've never seen a dragon. Unless it's a lizard.

503. All nursery rhymes have been sanitized for children and adults.

502. Its ok not to take a job if you don't like somebody in the corporation.

501. Its ok to take a job that you love as long as you love it but there are going to be days when you simply do not love your job.

500. If you have bone and muscle problems you are welcome to go out and buy castor oil to minimize the bone and muscle problems.

549. Money is a tool. Use it wisely.

548. There are more con artists in life than one knows what to do with.

547. Just because you think you are going to have an Unhappy Ending when you die doesn't mean it's true.

546. Happy Endings can be anything.

545. I love Happy Endings.

544. People have perverted filthy minds and will assume the worst about you. Don't believe their hype. They're just jealous.

543. Its ok to be homeless. You will find your way eventually even if it takes a little bit or a lot of time.

542. Becoming homeless is not good for the soul unless a person enjoys not having their own home.

541. Keeping people out of your life is a great thing to do. You should only keep the people in your life whom you want in your life. Toss everybody else out the door.

540. Having friends is not necessarily a good thing. "Friends will let you down, friends won't be around, All you need are friends." –Jodey Watley

539. Being happy all the time is impossible to do unless of course you want to act ignorant and don't mind being ignorant of all the other kinds of emotions you can also experience.

538. Its ok to put this book down and read it some other time. There's a lot of wisdom here and it's impossible to memorize all of the information here: take what you need and leave the rest.

537. There are cures for everything under the sun. If there isn't a cure then maybe you were born with a condition that will right it self at some point or this IS your life lesson. Work with living the best life you can despite your medical condition, etc.

536. Its ok to be mentally ill. Be glad that you are somebody. Being mentally ill isn't the worst stigma in the world: you don't even need to speak about what it means to be mentally ill: just live with the problem as best as you can and don't let it get the best of you.

538. The opposite of mental illness is mental happiness. Cherish it when you can be mentally happy and are able to act like that.

537. Yes means yes, no means no. Most people do not understand that and never will as they're lazy and would never admit to that either.

536. The temperature on The Other Side of Life is always 72*

535. Its ok to use your voice. Just remember to speak up when you need to and don't keep acting like a Victim: you were Born To Be Alive & to become a Victor.

534. What would you do if somebody came at you armed to the t??? Run like hell, meet your maker or ask them if they need a hug???

533. Its ok to have fun all the time: Nobody said you cannot have fun all the time.

532. Listening to music all the time is a good thing to do, especially when you are driving your car, your bike or doing something else. Otherwise, it might be better to study it. Music a gift from The Gods.

532. It's always great to be committed to finishing a project. If at some point you realize that you don't want to finish the project you can always abandon it and finish it later. You can also scrap the project permanently if this is really the way you feel about the project.

531. Some projects take a long time to finish. Others are finished in no time at all.

530. Some projects never get finished. That's just the way life is.

529. Doubting Thomas was exactly that. He thought way too much and had a massive case of low self-esteem. That's why they called him 'Doubting Thomas'.

528. Be thankful for Insurance.

527. Be thankful for hospitals.

526. Be thankful for hospitality.

525. Be a good host when you can remember to be a good host.

524. Its ok to make serious mistakes with your life. These mistakes only teach you to become stronger. Just make sure that you don't keep making the same mistake over and over and over and over and over again. You don't need that.

523. You can go for a walk anytime you like.

522. You can listen to any kind of music anytime you like.

521. Its ok to be you with all the range of emotions you contain.

520. You can choose to forgive all the people in your life or out of your life who have stepped all over you and left you high and dry for whatever reason. _______________________fill in the blanks.

519. You can choose to accept responsibility for everything that has ever happened to you in your lifetime. It's called forgiveness: let that one sink in and get all the sh*t out of your life: you'll feel better that you did.

518. When people treat you like sh*t they are also treating themselves like sh*t. You can choose to ignore that person's b.s. It's on them, not you.

517. You can choose to erase a lifetime of pain by simply walking away from all the abuse you have encountered along the way and you can choose to not dwell on it anymore as it will only end up getting in the way of who you truly are: A Beautiful Person.

516. When you cannot stop individuating about your past, you can choose to write down all the negative things people have done to you, i.e., trespasses and then make sure you are outside when you light it all on fire and let it go out of your life.

515. I choose to take responsibility for everything that has happened and that will ever happen to me with my life.

514. You can choose to end a friendship with anyone who doesn't agree with your way of life because you simply have had enough of that person's negative b.s.

513. Remember that a friend will let you down, a friend won't be around and that you can choose to not let your friends let you down. It's called boundaries. Develop them. Don't take what friends say to you personally. You can also choose to not be around that friend as they're a "toxic pain in the arse," anyways. Screw their b.s.

512. If you have such a hard time with living your life and the people who come and go in your life the best thing you can do is take a course or buy a book about "Assertiveness Training/Therapy". You can learn to say **NO** and **YES**. No means No, Yes means Yes, and, Maybe means "I will think about it." Sometimes that's your best answer.

511. Watching t.v. is good to do provided you limit yourself to 1 day a week. You have a busy life. Don't get addicted to the television. It's a massive time waster.

510. When people are being mean to you, overlook it and get out of their space as quickly as possible. They've shut down for whatever reason and you can choose to leave their personal space.

509. When a person walks all over you, why are they doing it? Stop them from doing it or just stop being around that person.

508. You can choose not to walk all over anybody in any way shape, form or fashion. It really doesn't get you or that person anywhere.

507. You can choose to develop boundaries when you are with or around people: that's the best course of action.

506. When somebody says, "I've had enough of you," get the clue and walk away from the person or stop doing what it is that you are doing that is irritating/bothering that person.

505. You can choose to be happy. There really isn't anything or anyone on this planet that can make you happy. Just be happy for the sake of being happy. That's the best anybody can do.

504. If you are possessed for any reason whatsoever, ask yourself the question: "Why am I possessed and what is really bothering me?"

503. When people are mad, let them vent. Don't take what they say personally. It will only end up affecting you personally and you don't want that.

502. Stop looking for your parents in other people. Your parents may owe you an apology but even if you confront them and they still believe the way they believe, don't take it personally. It's really not your fault that your parents can't forgive their parents and all the people who have screwed them over in their lifetime. That's just the way things work out sometime: it was never your fault the way they treated you growing up. Take responsibility for that thought alone and you'll feel so much better about what it means to have even been barely parented.

500. Some people no matter what you tell them are going to do whatever it is that they want to do. There is no stopping them from doing what they are going to do and don't even bother trying. They have to learn their own lessons the hard way or the easy way. It's not up to you to change people for who they are. Don't bother with that kettle of worms: it's simply not worth it to take another persons Inventory.

499. When it rains outside, you can go somewhere private, take off all your clothes and walk thru the rain in the nude. It's a very freeing thing to do. Try it sometime. It will be a good thing to do.

498. Nature IS the healer. Let Mother Nature heal you even when you don't know what to think about Mother Nature.

497. When somebody shows up at your home in the middle of the night, you can choose to not let them in.

496. When somebody decides they are going to victimize you there is nothing you can do about it. You can either ignore what they did or confront them or walk away and not let them victimize you. You can also choose to bring charges against them if what they did was so horrific that there is no other way around what did happen except by going through what happened.

495. When somebody throws "lemons" at you or life hands you "lemons" make lemonade.

494. There is nothing wrong with you. There never was. There never will be. You can choose to believe that there is something wrong with you thereby keeping going this "negative mental discourse" that you have going on inside your head or you can choose to put whatever is wrong with you to bed permanently. Put it in the 'Pandora's Box' or somewhere where it can hurt you not anymore. You don't deserve to be in years of pain. Nobody deserves that.

493. Being addicted to anything is a pain in the butt. Kick your addictions. When you cannot kick your addictions then you can always choose to get help for your addictions. Your addictions define who you are as a human being. Don't let your addictions control and ruin your life. You don't want that. You can choose to forgive whomever it is or whatever it is that you are doing that continues to make you do your addictions. That's called your "Emotional Pain Body".

492. When you were born, you were the most perfect you were when you came into this life. It's been quite a ride hasn't it???

491. When you die you will be your most perfect at the end of your life. You will be moving on to your next life if you believe in Reincarnation.

490. Everything else in your life is a cakewalk. Relish that thought.

491. When you get into an accident of any sort, you have to ask yourself, "Why was I not paying attention." You already know the answer. Don't ever let it happen again.

490. According to what I have heard from people over and over and over and over and over again: Accidents never happen in a perfect world, but, in this world, everything happens for a rea- son. Be glad you can choose to not let negative things happen to you AGAIN.

489. If there is something or someone that you need to let go of right now, just do it. You don't need any more emotional pain in your life. You really don't.

487. Chocolate cake is a wonderful thing to eat.

486. Vanilla cake is an even better thing to eat.

485. If you are allergic to anything in your diet, then don't eat it. Your body will thank you later.

484. If you are allergic to anyone then don't be around that person. Run like the dickens. Or, in real life avoid that person as much as you can. You can even choose not to speak to the person.

483. There never was anything wrong with you. It's all in your head. Best to stop thinking there is anything wrong with you. That kind of thinking doesn't get you anywhere anyways. It really doesn't.

482. Free your mind. Just free your mind. Everything else will follow.

481. Your past is your past. Let it stay in your past but don't think about it all the time or it will ruin your day to day life: you don't need the past sucking up all your good energy and zapping you of being happy all the time. You really don't.

480. There is love...

479. When a person or a group of people gives you thanks for whatever reason, be thankful and thank them for thanking you for your hard work, dedication and your blood, sweat & tears. Just accept the compliment(s). You owe it to yourself.

478. When somebody insults you can choose to not hear what they say and act like nothing happened. Or, you can laugh like you just heard a joke even if it's not funny. The person is not insulting you, they're insulting themselves and not being loving towards you or "Christian like," according to religious concepts.

477. It's really fun to be ALIVE: C E L E B R A T E your life every day of the year. Just do it!!! Life is a celebration, not a funeral.

476. There is nothing wrong with being a freak, a geek or a Social Outcast: That's who you are. Relish who you are as a human being, not as a Social Outcast.

475. I am a 'Spiritual Being Having A Human Experience'.

474. There is nothing wrong with being 'Gay'. This only means you are a happy person. Not necessarily a homosexual.

473. When people get all pissed off for any reason, it's not your fault. It's their fault. Don't take what they say or do personally. Just don't.

472. Its ok to be human. This is why you are here.

471. We are all made in Gods' image. This means we are all Gods and Goddesses. If you don't believe this statement then read up about "Creator Gods and Goddesses".

470. Some people who read #471 will choose not to believe what I just wrote. That's really their business. Let them believe what they want to believe and vehemently disagree with what I just wrote. It's their business. After all, this is just a book about becoming "more thankful". I didn't ask you to believe in every reason to be thankful.

469. Its ok not to believe in yourself. You will eventually even if that takes a long time to come to terms with. If you don't believe in yourself that's really your business. One day you will believe in you for no particular reason at all. You will feel grateful.

467. It's really ok not to believe in God. Or, the Devil. This only means that it hasn't been proven in that persons' mind that God/the Devil doesn't exist. It's called being 'Agnostic' or 'Atheist'. Some people choose to believe this their whole lives. Let them believe this. It's not your business to tell people to believe in 'God' as believing in God is **THE** hardest concept to understand. We may have all been made is Gods' image but from what I do know from the information that I have read, "We are created in Gods' eyes/image but we were created by more than one God." This I believe to be true for me. You are welcome

not to believe what I am writing here. Whole books have been written about this subject alone. In order for anyone to believe in God, some people need empirical proof that God does exist and since it is so difficult to believe in the idea of God/Goddess/Godhead it very easy to see how it would be difficult for anyone to believe in the existence of a God/God- dess/Godhead. In order to understand God better, you have to read up about God and all of the things that God has done for us as human beings having spiritual, emotional, psychological, physical, mental and etheric (chakras & nadis – ley lines in our body) experiences in their lives. Everybody is different and since there are no two people who are alike I choose to Celebrate my existence and I am glad that I exist as I am the idea and the embodiment of God/Jesus/Mary/Joseph and all of the disciples who previously lived to show us the way. A person can choose to believe in God or choose not to believe in God. That's a person's personal choice. You can choose to believe in yourself. We are all God looking at Gods' creation which is 'Planet Earth' and God would want us to believe in God and to choose to experience all that there is to experience in our minds, body, heart and soul. I am grateful. I choose to be grateful. I accept me in the present moment 100%. I love me for who I am, not for who other people think I should be/become. I choose to be happy, loveable and huggable me. I am made in Gods image and a reflection of God. I accept that part of me that is Godlike and of God. I also accept that part of me that is like the Devil for we all have God and the Devil Inside of Us. Science is better equipped to prove the existence of 'the god particle." Surely, not me. I'm no Scientist.

466. I am a beautiful person. So are you.

465. I believe in myself. It's best for me to believe in sweet, wonderful ME. Who else will believe in ME if I don't believe in ME??? Nobody!!!

464. I choose to be happy. I can be happy in the present moments.

463. I choose to be the embodiment of Jesus Christ as I was made for loving Jesus Christ. Jesus Christ was sent to Planet Earth to teach mankind many lessons. That it is possible to heal thy self and it is possible to heal people, places, animals and things. Jesus Christ may have been a martyr but he was a kind person who willingly went to his death. His death was the Ultimate Sacrifice for humanity. This he did for God/Goddess /Godhead/Humanity. I can't explain it any better than these words written on paper.

462. There is nothing wrong with you. There never was any- thing wrong with you. It really is all in your head: let all that garbage in your head be put into the compost pile or the garbage compactor. You don't need that stuff filling up your head anyways.

461. Your Body Is A Wonderland. Be grateful for that thought. I sure am.

460. When somebody decides to get even with you why did they do it in the 1st place? Did you do something to upset that person? Sometimes, you are Victimized for no particular reason at all. It's really not your fault. It happened. Let it go when you are able to let it go. You don't need **THAT!!!**

459. I am the happiest person on Earth as I choose to live by the teachings of Jesus Christ. Am I really the happiest person on Earth: when I remember the teachings of Jesus Christ. Just for your information: the Bible was written by a bunch of older wiser men.

Maybe some women also helped them write the book: that much I know is true.

458. I am happy that I can get out of bed in the morning and have a great day. I really am. So what it's miserable weather outside: that's just the way life is on Planet Earth.

457. Most people do not know what they have until it IS gone. Be grateful for what you have, not what you don't have. It's in the giving that we are healed.

456. When somebody chooses to trespass against you, you can choose to confront the person who crossed your boundaries. You might not get the answer you want and you may have to walk away from what that person did to you to upset your "Emotional Pain Body". You can choose to walk away or you can get even by getting what your idea of justice is in your eyes. This is up to you. If you are going to get mad and then get even there are more than 25 reasons for getting caught. Don't leave a trail if you are going to get even with the person who flipped you out and flipped you off. And, don't tell anybody either what you did. Just do it quietly and don't admit to any guilt when that person does confront you about what you supposedly did to get even with that person. Just don't give them any more ammunition than they already think they have. If that person chooses to yell at you, to get even with you or to physically harm you you have the right to defend yourself. Here in Maine, there is such a thing as **'Stand Your Ground'** which means you have the right to defend yourself to yours or the other person's death, worst case scenario. You really do. In other states, it's different. Find out what the laws in your state are telling you what you can do and what you can't do when it concerns protecting yourself and

your precious mind, body & Soul. You have the right to be here and to defend yourself and your possessions, etc. It's your God given right. You do what you have to do to keep yourself happy and safe at all hours of the day and night. It's your right!!! Just remember to leave God/Goddess/Godhead out of it.

455. The sun is always shining no matter when there are clouds in the sky or not. You just cannot see the sun shining up in the sky. That is all.

454. The moon is always reflecting the rays of light from the sun. Isn't that something? And, sometimes the moon and the sun are shining at the same time and you can see the both of them in the clear blue sky.

453. Sometimes, it's possible to see the Sun and the Moon during the day, as well as, at night, during an eclipse.

452. When it snows, be thankful for the fact that is it cold outside and that snow has a vibration all its own.

451. After a storm, sometimes a rainbow or even a double rainbow comes. That is just Nature making us happy after the storm and trying to show us "where the pot 'o gold really is."

450. If there were no storms, we'd all be insane in the membrain.

459. No matter what happens in your life, I will always believe in you. This is ME. This is why I wrote this book.

457. Choosing to believe in yourself is the most precious thing you can ever do. BELIEVING IN YOUR PRECIOUS SELF!!!

456. Its ok to have hate in your heart. It's a part of being human. Don't let it consume you or you may get mentally and/or physically sick from being too hateful, too spiteful, and too mean.

455. We are here because of desire. Our parents desire and love from what I've read.

454. According to what I have read, "All life is based upon Kharma & Dharma." We have all been here before. It's just that we are choosing to be here to experience our lives and the lives of other people. This is why we are here. Life is an amazing test. It's ok to fail every now and then or all the time. We keep fail- ing until we do succeed.

453. Its ok to fail your way through your life. Eventually, you will become calm and figure things out. Without failure, would you really know anything??? Yes you would: you would know what not to do the next time you encounter a failure in your life.

452. Its ok to be Ugly. Even Ugly is beautiful. Is it possible to be vain when one is ugly? I really don't know. Ugly IS the new Beautiful: you can't have one without the other.

451. Its ok to be Pretty. It just means you are beautiful and that you may be a woman. But, you might be a very vain person.

450. There are more things in life than one knows what to do with. Get rid of anything that you don't need in your life or that is busy taking up too much space in your existence.

449. Nobody owes you anything except all that they have stolen from you. It will be paid back to you in your next life. This is how life works. It's called Kharma & Dharma.

448. When a bird shits all over you what can you really do? Clean up that mess. You can choose to get mad about it but you can clean up that mess. Or, you can choose not to clean up that mess.

447. You can choose to decide who you do and who you don't let into your life.

446. Its ok to be a Bad Girl.

445. Its ok to be a Bad Boy.

443. If you are sad, find something or somebody to make you happy again and distract you from your "emotional pain".

442. If you are happy, be glad. You can choose to tell the whole world or you can just walk around with a smile on your face.

441. It's a lot of fun to cook. Be glad you can cook a meal for yourself or a group of people.

440. If you don't know how to cook, you can always choose to learn how to cook healthy meals for yourself by learning from a cookbook or letting somebody or a group of people teach you how to become a better cook.

439. If you decide to learn how to cook and still cannot master it then you can say, "I tried." Some things are not meant to work out in life. That's why t.v. dinners were invented: It's not a big deal or the worst thing that can happen to anybody. I know plenty of people who say they do not know how to cook.

438. When you are ready to move on, you will move on. Until that day, you may be stuck in misery. You can choose not to be miserable all of the time. Its' called "low self-esteem": it's a very common thing.

437. Misery loves company. If you are that miserable, you can choose to start your own pain group. Trust me, you will find people who feel exactly the way you feel and you will eventually need to move on from that group and let somebody else step in to run the group as it's much too much to carry on with the group.

436. You can choose to start so many groups in your life that you become a fearless leader. That's a plus. It really is.

435. Save all your feelings for **YOU, not somebody else who's going to try to ruin your life**. You don't need that.

434. You can choose to fall in love with somebody and when that person doesn't return your advances, then you can choose to get that person out of your life and you'll only end up finding somebody else who is exactly like that last person you did this to: **Solution**: find somebody who's not like you and don't force them into doing thing they're not ready to do. They'll pay attention to you when they're ready to pay attention to you: until then don't fret the small stuff. That's really how love works.

433. When somebody asks you for a favor, this only means that that person is too lazy to do what they need to do for themselves. Don't fall for it. Tell them to do whatever it is that they're too lazy to do for themselves or just leave. A person like this wants to be the director. That's all.

432. You can choose not to fall in love with anybody. Before you fall in love with somebody else fall in love with yourself. You'll be much happier that you did that 1st and then maybe you might want to fall in love with somebody else.

431. Sometimes, choosing not to fall in love with anybody is a great thing to do. This only means you are protecting your heart from being further damaged by people who tread all over you. If love doesn't work out for you in this lifetime, then it doesn't. I'm o.k. with that. I've been where you are right now: it's just not a pretty picture and I'm really done with love. I really am.

430. You can choose to be Onastic: Onanism is self-love and loving yourself the way you want to be loved. It's a great thing to do. Don't understand the word: look up the meaning of the word in a dictionary and find out what the word is related to and how it came into and why it came into being. That would be called etiology or how things come into being. Somebody bothered to make up that definition. **That's why we are here**: We are here to define ourselves and to love the world away. You can choose to love people, places, things and animals. You really can choose to be a lover of your own life. It's really all up to you how you see yourself in relationship to the whole wide world and people, places and things.

429. Writing a book like this is a daunting task: This book will eventually be done. "Thy will will be done". I choose to write a book like this as it is a book of hope and a 1001 Reasons to be grateful. That's another way of saying, "I'm thankful for what I have, and what I don't have." Sometimes, the only way to be is Neutral: when two people are asking you to take sides you can remain neutral or not get involved in their b.s.

It's not for you to resolve as you're not a "hostage negotiator". That's not your job anyways.

428. According to Elizabeth Kubler-Ross who survived the Nazi Death Camps, "There is no such thing as death." There is no need to prove it. Eventually, everything must die. This is the way of the world. If you are that obsessed with death & dying then read books about death and dying so that you understand a little bit more about death and dying and what it really means to be ALIVE & KICKING in this lifetime: this is your chance to understand your fear of death. We have all been there before when you believe in Spiritualism.

427. To everything turn, turn, turn...

426. Its ok to cry. Crying is a release of the Emotions: if a person doesn't cry what does this really mean??? They're holding in their Emotions and that's what could possibly make them sick and have a heart attack.

425. Big boys do cry.

424. Big girls cry.

423. Its ok to be super sensitive. This only means you need to shore up your ship and not let anything or anyone bother you. You can choose to be happy in the present moments. If you want to find out more about what it means to be a "super sensitive person" read this book: **The Highly Sensitive Person: How to Thrive When the World Overwhelms You – Elaine N. Aron Birch Lane Press, 1996.**

422. Live In The Present Moments: that's all that you really CAN DO: you'll be much happier for being and acting that way with your life: you

can learn to choose not to react to stupid people as they're all around us. They really are.

421. I have no past, no future. All I really have is **<u>NOW</u>**! I take advantage of the **HEAR & NOW!!!**

420. Some people say, "I have no past, no present, no future." **Live In The Present Moments**: that's all that you can really do. This is simply not true unless you believe you are '**The Walking Dead**'. However, being accepting of yourself is the best thing that you can do with your life. It really ***<u>IS</u>***!

419. You are here in this life because you want to be in this lifetime: take advantage of anything and everything and everybody that you can and be glad that you can be a happy person who lives in the present moments.

418. Living your life without **<u>Spice</u>** isn't such a bad thing especially when you don't want headaches. Some people just cannot handle spices in their diet. They just can't. I'm one of those people.

417. Chocolate tastes great and you can get high from eating it. Really high!!! Chocolate is basically a drug.

416. I learned a long time ago that when you are feeling frumpy the best thing that you can do is "Say Something Nice". It's also a song by Donna Summers from her double disc LP "Once Upon A Time".

415. Friends come & friends go. Some people aren't meant to be in your life for a very long time: they're like ships passing in the night. They really are.

414. A computer can be a blessing in disguise or a curse depending upon how you look at it: not everybody wants to be glued to their computer and cell phone 24/7. It's an addiction like anything else. You can choose when to be on the computer and when not to be on the computer. Cut the chord if you must.

413. When in doubt don't doubt. Ask questions and be thorough about what you're trying to get to the bottom of.

412. Donna Summer was a great singer. She started singing at the age of 3. Some people start singing at a really young age. Other people start singing when they're much older, wiser and more mature. That's just the way it is. Ex. Grandma Moses didn't start painting until she was 78 years of age. Isn't that an amazing tidbit or piece of information???!!!

411. Clouds come and clouds go. Doesn't mean it's going to rain. It might rain later.

410. The Illuminati call themselves the enlightened ones. I'm not so sure about that one. Anybody can choose to become "enlightened" at any stage of their life.

409. There is nothing wrong with you and if you think there is something wrong with you it might not necessarily be you causing the problem. Learn to listen to your body.

408. There are actors in the world and then there are actors. Who do you trust???

407. A person is using their 'Acting Voice' when they raise it up a few notches to control you. It's called their 'Speaking Voice'. Don't fall for

that trick. It's one of the oldest tricks in the book. You'll end up feeling used and abused: you don't want that.

406. When a storm comes through it comes through. Be glad nothing got ruined. Maybe you got rained upon. Not a big deal.

405. Sometimes, it's impossible to figure out when things are going to end. You can leave whenever you feel like you've had enough!!!

404. Hot Stuff can be anything.

403. Learning a musical instrument in front a crowd of people is one way to learn how to play. I highly recommend it. So what if people laugh. Putting out a receptacle or a hat for change might actually get you some money.

402. The MC doesn't always get things right: He or she is subject to making mistakes. This only means that the MC might not be doing their job. Sh*t happens, it really does.

401. When the sh*t hits the fan, you can always clean it up.

400. Unplugged doesn't mean you don't know how to play a musical instrument.

399. If it's too hot in your house, you can always turn down the heat AND open up the windows even in the dead of winter.

398. Becoming a Vegetarian isn't all that it is cracked up to be: You are subject to being addicted to sugar and being Vitamin B deficient. Make sure that before you decide to become a Vegetarian that you research as much information that you need to research to understand what

becoming a Vegetarian really involves so that you know what to eat and what not to eat.

397. There is always another day to get things straight with your life: just make sure that you don't wait 'til the last minute to organize your life and get things straight. You don't want that!!!

398. If somebody starts screaming at you you can always laugh at them and point them out with your finger. After they're done with having their fit then you can laugh some more and say something caustic to the person like, "Thanks for making me laugh mike hunt right off. That's the best entertainment I've had in years." Then walk away. I know, I know...

396. Its ok to die. Everything and everyone has to die e v e n t u a l l y...

395. Its ok to live your life. It really is: just learn to say, "NO," and "go love yourself," when you're in a position that you don't want to be in. That's **THE BEST THAT YOU CAN DO** anyways.

394. Its ok to move to a different venue if the current one isn't working out for you anymore. It really is...

393. People are very nice when they want something out of you. Then they slither away like a snake in the grass. What's up with that? See point #395 AGAIN!!! Memorize those two valuable lines written JUST FOR YOU!!! That's why I wrote this book.

392. People are exceptionally nice to you for the following reasons: **1.** to get something from you, **2.** to call you and bug you about wanting to talk your ears off, **3.** to borrow something they are going to refuse to return and when you remind them of it they come up with excuses

about returning what you loaned them. **"Neither A Borrower Nor Lender Be**." It's best to get a job that you like doing: otherwise, you're not helping your cause whatsoever. -**Shakespeare**

391. When you are so depressed you want to commit suicide make sure that you call somebody to speak to them about why you feel the way you do. If you do commit suicide you're not helping your cause and you'll only end up coming back in another body under similar circumstances as you simply did not learn your lessons in this lifetime. Here are some numbers: 1-800-273-8255, Maine Crisis Hotline: 1-888-568-1112. There's ALWAYS somebody who cares even when you don't think so.

390. Say a little prayer. It may just help you to get what you want out of your life. At the very least it will help you to feel better about yourself. You might not get what you want but at least you'll be feeling better from having said a little prayer to help you get through your life.

389. It takes a lifetime to live your life: Don't rush anything. There is plenty of time to grow and become the person you need to become.

387. So you think you're going to become famous??? '**A Legend In Your Own Mind**,' is more like it. Go for it. Be prepared to work your butt off to get what you want.

386. You may not be the sharpest tool in the shed but you don't need to be a sharp tool in order to get your point across. That's not how it really works: sometimes, you just want to sit and listen to people and make them wonder who you are and not say a word until the time is right.

385. You can always go for a really long walk. And, it's not off of a short pier either. If you throw yourself off the pier you better make sure that you are ready to swim back to shore.

384. **Make Believe**, that's what I do to get me through…

383. If you're not satisfied ever this only means you have strict standards. Loosen up a little bit and be glad you are so good at the things you choose to do with your life: you are **THE BEST!!!** Why expect anything less???!!!

382. This _IS_ your life. Enjoy it while you still can. There may come a day when you cannot do anything but be complacent and agreeable to get what you want. Doesn't mean that you will land in a Nursing Home, an Assisted Care Facility, a Group Home, a Hospital, a Rehab, etc.

381. You can always climb a tree at any age even if you need someone or something to help you get in that tree.

380. Its ok to love yourself. It really is ok. Nobody says that you can't. Saying that you can't is not the right words to use ever unless you are the Boss: then anything you say or do goes: and, it's not as I say or do: let's us just help each other get the job done in a calm manner.

379. Love happens to you over and over and over and over and over again. Be prepared for it when it does happen. When it doesn't happen then what you do you do???!!! Just sit and wait for it to come back: it'll come back…eventually…

378. Sh*t Happens. Deal with it when it happens. Doesn't mean that you are a bad person. It's just The Shit hitting the fan: clean up as best as you can…

377. Expect good things to happen in your life.

376. For every bad thought you have, think of something positive that will make you happy.

375. Life is a Comic Tragedy. Deal with it as best as you can and don't spread yourself too thin. That's not a great thing to be doing.

374. When there is nothing left to believe in there is always sweet incredible you to believe in. That's enough.

373. It's never too late to pick up a Musical Instrument.

372. Doubting Thomas. Why was he so popular and so famous in the afterlife???

371. It's ok to work every day of your life likes it's your last day on Earth.

370. Finishing things is a great thing to do. This means you had your eye on the prize all the time.

369. Sugar is the bane of all poets. And, other people, as well.

368. There are 3 ways to organize things alphabetically: in sequence from A – Z or backwards from Z- A or haphazardly. Whatever floats the boat to get the job done: you can always choose to get super organized later on down the road.

367. You can also organize everything in your life according to type, size and feel. If you were raised by a hoarder I truly understand what you are always going through: best to get organized when you can do it and are up to the challenge of getting rid of things. Just make sure that you

make 3 separate piles: **1.** Junk pile **2.** Garbage **3.** Stuff to sell or give away.

366. It's ok to go for a walk even in the middle of the night: Maybe you just cannot sleep and are deficient in nutrients. You can also eat food to fall asleep if you must. Don't worry about gaining weight. And, don't think too much about how the food will keep you up all night because food does give you energy when you eat it. You can always buy yourself a box of earplugs to help you get to sleep at night, listen to music or drink some alcohol as I know of a ton of people who do this as alcohol is a sedative anyways. Whatever it takes to get to sleep at night is what you need to do with **YOU**!!!

365. When somebody interrupts your space, keep pressing on. If the thought comes back that's great, if it doesn't just ask the person you are with what you were talking about before you rudely got interrupted.

364. If you are comfortable with being abused emotionally and physically you really have to ask yourself what you get out of being treated like sh*t. Some people have such low self esteem. So they go around treating other people like sh*t because they have a grudge to bear they haven't quite worked through yet.

363. Seek Professional Help when necessary and do not be afraid to ask for Professional Help. You just may need the help in every way possible.

362. A map is sometimes a great thing to own. They're great for long distance trips: bring one with you anyways even though you have a cell phone that can do the same thing.

361. Sometimes, you just might want to throw the map out the car window. Don't do it unless you are sure you want to do it. You might have to turn the vehicle around to pick it up off the road as you find out you really do need that map to get to where you need to go.

360. Thousands of people help you to get what you need with your life. Be glad that there are people in your life at all. Unless of course, you like being away from people days at a time.

359. Sometimes, you want to dress like a homeless person. Ain't nothing wrong with that. Sometimes, you just want to look like a million bucks. Go for it! Who's to stop you from feeling great about yourself???!!!

358. Homeless people need love: They cannot be blamed for their circumstances. They really can't.

357. Blame, Shame & Guilt don't really get you anywhere with your amazing life. Keep that stuff to a minimum.

356. You can always choose to go to Walmart to shop until you drop. Somebody will pick you up if you fall on the floor.

355. Its ok to feel like nobody cares about you at all. This only means that you must 'Take Care' like people keep telling you to do when they say goodbye to you after a conversation is over.

354. Sometimes somebody doesn't want to talk to you even though it looks like they do. Respect that boundary. You can always find somebody else to talk to. There are over 7 billion people in this world.

353. Non-Verbal Communication is much more important than Verbal Communication ever was or is.

352. When you get sick of listening to the music you listen to you can always choose to turn it off or get rid of it permanently or sell it, etc. Music is meant to be shared anyways. Share it when you feel like it. Sharing means caring.

351. Sometimes, moving South is just what the doctor ordered. Doesn't mean that you cannot come back to where you used to live to check out the scene once again. Nobody says you need to be the "center of talk" all the time: that's no way to live your life. This only means that you didn't get enough love as a child? I reallydon't know what your circumstances are.

350. I love 'Happy Endings' in more ways than the obvious one.

349. Madonna and other people famous and not so famous only eat half of what they put on their plate. That's one way to keep weight off. Doesn't mean you are a bad person when you eat too much food. Maybe you have a "high metabolism". Eat foods that bring you up, not bring you down.

348. Its ok to be sad, mad, glad and bad all at the same time. I won't think any less or any more of you.

347. **R-E-S-P-E-C-T** show you what it means to me, take care, tcb…

346. Its ok to keep doing your addictions until you get sick of doing them and find another way out: nobody says you need to listen to your "emotional pain body" all the time: that's the source of your addictions.

345. Going to any **Self Help Group** is ok to do but beware of getting addicted to going to the meetings all the time. Some people go every day for 100 days then say, "what the h*ll was I thinkin." You only need

to do something like that when you are not able to let go of your "emotional pain body" as that what keeps the addictions going: maybe you should work your way through why you are in pain instead of being in pain all the time.

1. I'm allowing myself to heal by
Living in the present moment(s)

2. I can choose to live my life &
not do my addictions

3. I don't need any excuses not to
like myself as I get enough
negative b.s. from the old tapes
(blame) running thru my head
and people who think they're my
boss.

4. Freedom vs Love — freedom to
be myself & love me & who I
choose to love. That's my business

5. I forgive God, myself &
the people I've be hurt me, etc.

I love & care for myself as
best I can 24/7

totally unconditionally

344. A computer can always be replaced when it breaks down: maybe the next computer you want to buy will be a refurbished computer: if it breaks down within a year you can keep getting it replaced by the company that made it for you. Or, just buy a brand new one that isn't refurbished.

343. A cell phone can definitely be replaced. And, you don't need an 800 cell phone to check your food stamp balance. You really don't.

342. I've never lost a cell phone yet and don't plan on it. It's just a matter of prioritizing what I want in my life.

341. When someone is trying to pressure you into buying something you can always say, "I'll think about it." Then walk away. Maybe you just aren't ready to spend that kind of money yet???!!!

340. Eating food regularly 3 times per day will make you very fat. You mite want to consider eating 6 small meals per day or eating one meal a day and two small meals.

339. Some people have to constantly eat to stay alive. What's up with that???!!!Be glad that you're not in that position.

338. This Time I Know It's For Real. It really is.

337. "I'm going crazy." I must ask myself what is really making me crazy. Could it really be me or something in my environ- ment??? You just never know what the answer might be.

336. I'm great at making myself feel guilty but I don't have to play that game all the time. Guilt is the worst thing in the world: it leads to blame and shame: you don't want that. Has nothing to do with religion. It's just the way people are built.

335. If your hands and feet are dry, put some lotion on them that is healthy for you and not loaded full of parabens, dyes and other chemicals, etc. etc. Go Organic even when it costs you more money. It's definitely worth it.

334. Olive Oil is great for your complexion. So is coconut oil. Use them wisely.

333. Coconut Oil is great for a lot of conditions including your hair, your face, your hands, your feet, cancer, weight loss, etc.

332. When was the last time you really did love yourself??? Don't answer that question unless you need to right now.

331. Its ok to make typos on a paper that has to be turned in for grading. Doesn't mean that you're going to fail the class. You'll just end up getting a lower grade and have to do much better on your next paper. You wan't to make sure that you get the best grade possible not to impress the teacher but to impress yourself.

330. When someone tries to control, manipulate and dominate you: you can always choose to control, manipulate or dominate that person and then when things keep going South between the two of you, you can always choose to walk away and forget about that person for a while or even forever. It's called boundaries. Use boundaries to get what you want out of your life. Create WIN/WIN Situations with your life.

329. Some people can't even open their eyes as they are blind for life. Be glad that you are not one of these people. But, they can still see. What's up with that???!!!

328. You can open your eyes and close them any time you want to. Make sure to be grateful for being ALIVE in this place & time. You are meant to be HERE NOW!

327. You can open your eyes and go right back to bed when you want to but don't get in the habit of sleeping in unless you want to and you don't need to go to work. Sleeping too much will put pressure on your body and make you a "heavy" person.

326. Your eyes have it. But, not all eyes have it. I know, I know: not all of us were meant to be born with eyes that draw attention to us.

325. The eyes are the window to the soul. For some people.

324. My Eyes Adored You – Frankie Valli & The Four Seasons

323. Eyes That See In The Dark – Kenny Rogers

322. You have a close personal circle of friends: everybody does. Be glad that you can speak to anybody.

321. Some people will love you no matter what. Some people are not ready to. They might never be ready to or it just isn't meant to be: C' est la vie, that's just the way it goes.

320. You are meant to be **HERE NOW**!!!

319. You can listen to anything you like at any time of the day or night.

318. Choosing the 1st person you fall in love with to have a relationship with is not a wise thing to be doing: what if the relationship doesn't work out: then what???!!! Choose wisely who you will live with and marry...eventually...if you keep making mistakes what's the lesson???!!!

317. It's possible to live in other parts of the Universe. It really IS...that's right: I'm a 'Conspiracy Theorist'. I really am. I don't care what people think of me either. I'm not here to kiss people's a**e* with my needing to accepted, wanted or loved.

316. None of Us are from **Planet Earth**: from what I know Spiritually as everything was physically brought HERE!!!

315. It's possible to keep ones mouth shut and not inflict more pain & suffering on other people. That's what **R E S P E C T** is called these days. Try it sometime: it doesn't cost a dime.

314. When somebody doesn't like you it's not your respon- sibility to get upset with their b.s.: just try to ignore it as best as you can and if you're going to quit a job because that person's voice sets you off you can always ask for a transfer to a subsidiary of the company. You really can. Don't just quit unless you know you can't take that person's vibrations anymore and there are no other options. Be wise about the situation.

313. It's a beautiful day outside even when it does rain.

312. You can eat whatever you like even if that means you're going to be on the reality show **'My 600lb. Life'**.

311. You can call me anything you like but don't call me late for dinner!!!

310. Whenever you get pissed off you can vent to somebody as there's always somebody who will listen to you. If there isn't anybody available then you can always get out the punching bag and take it out on the punching bag.

309. You can always call somebody you know and talk their ears off to resolve problems in your mind: that's what friends are for. But, if you keep talking about the same problem all the time this only means you need to let it go. The problem isn't going to get you anywhere by talking about it all the time.

308. You can listen to **Tibetan Bells** music to calm down.

307. You can listen to **Ambient Space** music that will help you to feel better about yourself and where you are headed with your gorgeous life. Some of that stuff is called a 'solfeggios'. It's another kind of music set a different vibrations to help you heal like 737 hertz, etc.

306. When it's raining outside you can go walking in the rain and smell the dew on the ground or after it rains: it's quite an intoxicating smell isn't it??? It's the next best thing next to sex and having it.

305. When Mr. Blue Sky comes back it's a reason to put on any ELO record.

304. When it's below zero you must remember to become very grateful & thank yourself for being **ALIVE!** Make sure that you bundle up before going outside. & make sure that you wear your gloves, scarf & hats outside as it's going to be very nippy out there and you don't want frostbite!!!

303. You don't live with your parents anymore: you moved out years ago: just make sure that you don't end up in a relationship with your parents as it won't work out with the two of you. It just won't unless you accept the lessons that being in a relationship with somebody who reminds you of your parents teaches you.

302. You don't speak to any of your relatives as they're all relative in the scheme of things: so what: you don't need their issues. You really don't. It's just not meant to be.

301. You can pretty much go anywhere you want to when you need to and when you can't you can ask a good friend to help you out to get where you need to get with your life.

300. When in doubt sus it out!!!

299. There is such a thing as **FREE CARE** in America: take advantage of it & don't have any shame about not being able to pay the bill off in time: that's called Insurance. Insurance Companies are one of the biggest scams ever created to suck money out of people's wallets.

298. When it's the middle of the nite and the birds are chirping in the middle of the nite @ 3:OOAM what do you do: be grateful that you're alive and that you own a bed you can sleep in without being disturbed in the middle of the night when it's the weekend.

297. You can make a decision to purchase a brand new car or a shite car: I'll take the brand new vehicle any day of the week or the showroom model used for demonstration purposes.

296. You can make the decision to get rid of anything that you haven't used for at least 6months to a year!!!

295. Letting go of things is much easier to do when you leave them in a box beside the road, leave them in somebody's hallway or throw them in the trash or call up your nearest "**Donation Center**" to schedule a time to pick that crap up or just leave it in the hallway for them to come and take at their leisure!!!

294. Just because you're in love with an addict doesn't mean that you have to get mad at them because they won't put out: maybe you should just tighten your purse strings and let that person go. Don't give them what they want: money. You don't need any more DRAMA from them. Just **LET THEM GO!!!**

293. It's fun to write a book that has 1001 Ways To Be Thankful & get closer & closer to finishing the darn thing.

292. Be grateful that you have fish in your fish tank that are still living: make sure you change the filter and the water at least one time per month and don't get a whole bunch of fish just to find out that you've got an aggressive fish in the tank killing all of the fish. That's not the way to make a fish tank succeed: the best thing you can do is buy Community Fish vs. Aggressive Fish for your brand new or used tank. Also, make sure that you read up about the taking care of a fish tank before you buy the darn thing: that's what I'd do with my next fish tank.

291. Just because you are **ALIVE** doesn't mean that you can't be THANKFUL for the fact that your body breathes you every day of your life.

290. When was the last time that you felt THANKFUL: **GIVE THANKS RIGHT NOW** if you feel like it!!!

289. You cannot use God to judge other people: that's not the way it works. Leave The Bible out of it. PLEASE I BEG OF YOU!!!

288. Listening to Pop Muzik might just be the best thing for you right now as any kind of music will relax you and make you feel better. Well, almost any kind of muzik…

287. Just because the temperature is -70* doesn't mean that you can't step on your back porch if you have a back porch.

286. When somebody says, "Praise Be, Praise Thou," I sure hope they're being serious and not religious on me.

285. When you find out that one of your relatives has passed on it's a great time to say, "It's about time and crack open a few beers to C E L E B R A T E their passing. Mourn them if you must, but make sure that you say something kind & positive about them and then let them go."

284. Sometimes, the best thing you can do is go for **W A L K** <u>or even a</u> **RUN, RUN, RUN** <u>thru the neighborhood</u>. Mite as well get in shape if you're that depressed and you need exercise.

283. Just because somebody says they're your friend doesn't mean they are: put them to the test. Really make them your friend. So what the two of you fight every now and then: that's o.k. as really good friends will go to the ends of the Earth for each other or will they??? Hmmm…I just opened up a can of worms.

282. You can do anything that you set your mind & heart to.

281. Sometimes instead of acting with Anger it's much easier to ask the person yelling at you if they need a hug…

280. Just because your parents are not in your life anymore doesn't mean that you need to keep harping on them about things that happened so long ago. None of it was your fault anyways: just be glad that you got away from their nasty b.s. & that you're a FREE MAN.

279. Sometimes the best thing that you can do is kiss the ground that you walk on especially after a near fatal accident.

278. When somebody tries to tell you what to do you have to question that persons **AUTHORITY**: do you really want to do what that person is telling you to do??? If not, don't do it.

277. When you can't get along w/ any of your relatives be grateful: maybe it's time to just separate **PERMANENTLY** to avoid any more confusion with them. A lot of us don't want to be reminded of our past and it really does hurt inside. So what!!! Love is not supposed to hurt unless you like being beaten up on a regular basis...

276. Has anybody seen Casper The Friendly Ghost lately??? I haven't.

275. When it gets too cold in your home you can always go out and buy a 40 heater from a discount store in your area. That will really help with keeping you WARMER especially if you live in a very large home.

274. You can also put plastic on your windows so that your home is nice, toasty & warm as it gets downright colder in New England. Or, you can just pack everything up and get the f out of dodge permanently and go live somewhere where it's hot & muggy all the time...

273. When somebody gives you a hard time you can choose to acknowledge what that person is doing but don't get upset when you can help yourself. You won't get anywhere with yourself or other people by having a "trantrum" and people will think that you've definitely lost your mind.

272. Just because somebody says they want to do something with you doesn't mean that they're going to follow through with what they say they're going to do with you: don't believe everything that people tell you. As a matter of fact, ,make sure that you confirm a really big trip somewhere before you go so you can know and don't do it by .txt as

that's not the way to do business. I learned that one the very hard way: now, I'm not friends with this person: they're on my "permanent burn list."

271. Be Glad That You Are ALIVE & you can use Google to call people up on the computer and get FREE PHONE CALLS & not have to ask somebody to use their phone. Think about all the money you'll be saving by using GOOGLE to make FREE PHONE CALLS when you need to speak to somebody on the phone and you don't want to waste your call time with your limited cell phone. **THINK ABOUT IT!!!**

270. Insurance is a blessing when you need to use it so use it carefully.

269. There is such a thing as 'Life After Life' but I just didn't just say that!!!

268. Can you imagine how limited your life might be if you had one of your senses missing or limited: it happens to the best of us…Stevie Wonder last I knew of had only two of his senses working correctly. He's an amazing person. So are YOU!!! Stevie was in an serious car accident August 6, 1973. He was already blind from birth thanks to getting too much oxygen when he was in the incubator at the hospital where he was born. He lost his sense of smell, temporarily lost his sense of taste. At that point he basically became a walking pair of ears. We have 6 senses: eyes, ears, taste, touch, smell and psychic abilities which differ with everybody.

267. When was the last time you went to see a very good concert by your favorite recording Artist?

266. When was the last time you went to a Festival?

265. Things really haven't changed all that much since times of Ancient Lore: we just have a lot more stuff to keep us occupied as far as electronics go. After all, we are living in the 21st Century: The Age of Enlightenment

264. You can always **<u>DELETE</u>** YOUR facebook, twitter, Instagram, & tumbler accounts if you're that sick of Social Media and being addicted to it or you could just limit yourself to one time per week or month.

263. You can always become an Influencer thru Instagram and become an Instagram Star of the moment. Trust me, there will be other people to fill your shoes.

262. A ruler is always a good thing to have around and not just for obvious reasons.

261. Just because you own a cell phone doesn't mean that you can't turn it off at night when you go to bed. You don't want to walk around being "sleep deprived now do you???!!! **MAYBE**

260. Just because you own a computer doesn't mean that you have to be on it 24/**7**: take breaks every now and then.

259. You can always do hand and foot exercises right before you get on your computer for at least 5 minutes during the day and more to make sure you don't have to have your fingers fixed with the doctor: that's a really great route to take: E X E R C I S E!!!

258. You can always get rid of your landline but make sure that you want to do that and that you've thought it thru and what your backup phones are going to be when the Internet goes out on you or you forget to pay your bill on time: it happens to the best of us.

257. If somebody wants to be on your cell phone plan is that really a good idea: especially when that person is an addict: think that one thru carefully. Been there, done that: NO CAN DO!!!

256. Sometimes, scaling back what you actually own is the best thing you can do.

255. Just because you say NO to somebody and they get pissed off at you doesn't mean that you need to get upset: it was never about you, it was about them and their addictions.

254. An ice cold beverage is sometimes the best course of action. Not necessarily a beer or a stiff drink. Sometimes, you just want to lay off the HARD STUFF!!!

253. Just because you like somebody doesn't mean they want a realationship with you: deal with that on a Mature Level not an Immature Level: there is a difference. There REALLY is: think about it: do you want that level of crazy in your life anyways: I think not!!!

252. There are more fish in the sea to fry so why get upset when somebody leaves you: maybe it just wasn't meant to be and you WERE BEING USED: you knew that all along but you just didn't listen to yourself. Better Luck Next Time Baby!!!

251. Just because somebody tells you that you cannot do something doesn't mean that you can't do it: tread very carefully and be glad that that person is not in your life anymore: they had no right to mess you up emotionally/psychologically/physically like that: it's not right for people to do that but it happens all the time. Be very careful what and whom you listen to these days: some people are wearing clothes they shouldn't be wearing and bearing false witness against you and this is a

crime against humanity and should not be. But, it happens all the time. Don't keep making that simple mistake.

250. Around The World In 80 Days

249. Sometimes, the best thing you can do is say something funny to ease the tension in the room: maybe you want to introduce yourself to the whole room of people or just crack a joke or ask anybody if they have any jokes they'd like to crack at you just to get the ball rolling. It all depends on what kind of a group you are forming.

248. There's nothing wrong with you: there never was anything wrong with you to begin with. That's where you go wrong every day of the week, etc.

247. Sometimes, it's very nice to sit in your room NAKED & not worry about much of anything.

246. Sometimes, answering the door NAKED is the best thing to do. So what you're making whomever is at your door nervous: there are worse things that could happen on any given day of the week.

245. Sometimes, just meeting a person for a few seconds is all that you really need: a SMILE, a WINK & a NOD...who knows what will happen next time...

244. Sometimes you want to keep your fingers crossed just in case things don't work out. Hell, you know if a job is going to work out, a relationship, a landlord, etc. You really do: get used to listening to that little voice inside yourself. It can mean the difference between a hellish life and a life of relaxation and happiness: don't make decisions that you're going to regret!!!

243. Be glad that the people who abused you while growing up are not in your life anymore to take advantage of you emo- tionally, psychologically and physically: you really don't need that shite anymore. You really don't.

242. Are We Our Selves???!!!

241. Sometimes, somebody doe s save your life. Be Grateful they stepped in at the right moment.

242. Sometimes, you end up saving somebody's life: be grateful that you were able to help somebody through their own mistakes.

241. Keep making mistakes until you get it right: you'll eventually exceed all expectations: sometimes it's really not about **Great Expectations**. That was a book that was written quite some time ago: not all of us have to become great for something that we do: we can just accept what we do for what it is, not necessarily what we want it to be.

240. I write the songs that make the young girls sing, I write the songs of love and special things because my name is Barry Manilow! I also write the songs for young boys, as well. Why did I take so long to come out???

239. I keep writing this book: will it ever be finished??? I sure hope so: my arms are getting tired from all this typing: maybe I ought to take a big break: there, now I feel better.

238. Sometimes the best thing that you can do is ask people if they believe in JESUS. After all, he was a martyr and you don't want to become a martyr for your own cause or do you??? Maybe

237. Light is the key according to Architecture & making any kind of Art.

236. B E L I E V E in something!!!

235. When you finally buy a brand new vehicle make sure that there are no defects in it by doing your job of vetting that vehicle out through a Consumer Agency, etc. You definitely don't want a lemon.

234. When somebody hands you lemons what do you do???!!!

233. You can test people to find out if they're HONEST by leaving a dollar bill on the floor.

232. You can go to sleep at night knowing that you've always done your best work even when it wasn't good enough.

231. If it's really that rainy outside you can always use your Umbrella.

230. If it's raining and pouring the old(er) man may be snoring but you can always put in your ear plugs if you don't want to hear his snoring as it's driving you crazy.

229. If It's raining and pouring outside like cats & dogs you might want to consider putting on a raincoat, rain pants & rain shoes. How wet do you want to get by the time you get to where you need to go??? I dunno!!!

228. When somebody says JUMP don't get alarmed: ask them HOW HIGH DO YOU WANT ME TO JUMP???!!! That'll make them think twice about being mean to you.

227. When you can't find something in your computer you don't need to get upset: maybe it will turn up later on at the correct time: just be patient.

226. The best thing you can do is not be possessive with anybody: what will that get you but more grief???!!!

225. The sun will come out tomorrow bet your bottom dollar, tomorrow, tomorrow, it's a brand new day.

224. When your son or daughter comes out to you the best thing you can do is accept them for who they are. Their sexuality is not about you anymore: it really isn't.

223. There's nothing wrong with being GAY. As a matter of fact, that word used to mean HAPPY back in the day. Now it just means homosexual: what is a homosexual anyways: yes, I got you to say that word: MY BAD!!!

222. Has anybody ever watched the program Room 222: I did as a kid?

221. FABULOUS is a great word to use and not just around gay people. Use it all the time.

220. Just because somebody is mad at you doesn't mean that you won't ever talk to them again: it just means they're getting their panties in a twist. The storm will pass soon enough.

219. Just because somebody asks you for a favor doesn't mean that you have to do whatever it is that they are asking you to do. They're just being very lazy with you as they don't want to get up, etc. Not your problem. Make them get up: it's all about being controlling for them, it really is.

218. If somebody says that you look FAT don't take it personally: maybe they're suffering from shoveling too much food in their mouth all the

time. Time to move on and not take things so seriously with what anybody says…

217.

216. Just because the moon is so far away doesn't mean that you can't frame it with your fingers and catch it like a rising star in the night sky.

215. Having FFUN FFUN FFUN is what it's all about with ME…I like having fun no matter who I am with. Try it sometimes. It really works.

214. Love The One You're With

213. Sometimes the best thing you can do is STEP ON YOUR LIPS. You know saying the wrong combination of words will makes things much worse than they are so why do it???!!! If you're in a position that you don't want to be in you can always scream bloody murder or RAPE: that's your choice: you want to survive the situation, not become a statistic.

212. A friend in need is a friend indeed

211. SMILE when you're so down & sad that you don't think you can make it on through. Together We Can Make It and if we try we can get by…

210. Love Makes The World Go 'Round

209. Aren't you glad that you are ALIVE & KICKING, stay until your love is, love is…?

208. Just because somebody told you that you CAN'T doesn't mean that you CAN'T DO IT: just do it anyways when it means that much to you.

That's how all of us learn anyways: you'll find out if it's meant to be done by succeeding or not...

207. Writing & Research is the best thing that you can do especially when it concerns saving money.

206. Sometimes suing a big giant deceptive corporation IS the best thing that you can do.

205. Make Amends When You Can and it's going to make a situation better.

204. Sometimes, making amends just won't do and it's only going to make the situation worse than it already IS so why bother???

203. Loose lips sink big ships so be careful not to open your mouth if you can avoid it.

202. Loose lips sink really big ships: is this what you enjoy doing or can you just mind your own business for once???

201. Just because somebody threatened you with a bad time doesn't mean that you need to take that person seriously.

200. Just because Mama says you can't do it doesn't mean that Dada will approve either: may as well ask both parents what to do. Have a "group meeting". They'll wonder what the 'f is going on with you.

199. When neither one of your parents will support your idea then maybe it's time to just ignore them and do what needs to be done anyways. You just might end up surprising everybody...

198. I can do anything that I set my mind to, I really <u>CAN</u>!!!

197. Just because you got a bad review of your book online doesn't mean that you need to take that person to heart: maybe they're just a cruel, mean vindictive beatch: that's not your problem. People are going to judge you whether you like it or not: ignore them: they're critics anyways and you don't need to be reading every review made against you.

196. Sometimes, the best thing you can do is put an ad in the newspaper and ask somebody to take you to Six Flags and pay for gas and a meal, etc. You'll be glad that you did THAT!!! I highly recommend riding rollercoasters at any time of the year.

195. Sometimes, that happy place isn't so far off: it could be going to your favorite fast food restaurant and pigging out, an 'All You Can Eat Buffet' or to a 'Community Gathering'.

194. Sometimes, that happy place is inside your heart.

193. Sometimes, people don't know when to stay out of your business: that's the reality of being HUMAN: you can always place a "Protection of Abuse" or "Cease Harassment Order" on that person or group of people who refuse to leave you ALONE & MIND THEIR OWN BUSINESS: just make sure that it's the right thing to do.

192. Sometimes a very long break from something that you really care about is the best thing that you can do: but don't take what you did personally and over analyze what you do as being wrong.

191. There's already enough Blame, Shame & Guilt in this world: don't worry about anything that is not your concern.

190. A hoagie is a great kind of sandwich to eat at any time of the day or night.

189. Sometimes, it's great to go walking late at night in your neighborhood NAKED IN THE WOODS.

188. If you are that bored you can always move on to something else to keep you busy. You've got a lot of work to do with your life so why get upset about anything: make sure that when you work on projects that are important to you that you take small, baby steps to get things done: no sense in stressing yourself out about what you are doing with your life.

187. Ice Cream is a gift from the Gods. **Cherish** it!!!

186. Sometimes, a geographical cure is exactly what you need with your life. Just move away and don't ever look back.

185. **BECAUSE** is definitely an answer

184. Why did you cross that bridge??? BECAUSE IT WAS THERE!!!

183. Sometimes you want to pray: just get down on your hands and knees and start PRAYING!!!

182. Sometimes even though it's not a nice thing to tell somebody you can say the words, "You're An ASSHOLE." When they get upset all you have to do is say, "Did I just step on my lips." Then walk away. You don't need that person's NEGATIVI- TY!!!

181. STOP! is a great way to say, "I'm going to do something else for a while and then get right back to what I was doing."

180. When somebody says, "GO," you might be playing Red Light, Green Light…

179. Does anybody know what a lug wrench is??? MAYBE like the GEICO commercial says

178. What exactly is a Pain In The Neck??? A person, a pain in your neck or something that you just can't figure out???!!!

177. Back in the day before electricity was invented people worked from sun up to sun down: be glad that you have enough electricity to power your computer, cell phone & other electronic gadgets.

176. Sometimes, a Solar Charger is exactly what you need to get the job done!!!

175. 1776 is the day America was LIBERATED: July 4th to be precise!!!

174. Columbus didn't discover America: it was really the Indians. It was actually American Vikings but let's give credit where credit IS DUE: the Indians were here long before any of those settlers where here.

173. When all else fails, "What would Jesus do???"

172. Sometimes LOVE comes from unexpected places

171. Forever GRATEFUL.

170. What does INFINITY mean to YOU, sweet wonderful YOU!!!

169. What's your favorite set of numbers???

168. Don't be a Spoil Sport when you can help it.

167. Listen to your favorite music when you don't think that you can go on…it will help to motivate you do move on in the direction you need to go in.

166. Namaste: I honor the SOUL & SPIRIT that is YOU!!!

165. Will robots really take over the world??? Depends on the job field they're made for.

164. What is Armageddon?

163. What is a Modern Man?

162. No Moving Parts Inside: what could I possibly be???!!!

161. with Parts Made In Japan

160. What was life like before paper, toilet paper, outhouses, running water and electricity???

159. What is your favorite number???

158. Be glad that you can count back from 100 when you can't get to sleep at night.

157. If you don't want to backward from 100 you can always count sheep with Little Beau Peep!

156. I'm Alive is an answer

155. God is good, God is great, God loves it when I …

154. From what I've heard Goddess made this Universe: actually, it was The Creator Gods so I'd believe in Creationism.

153. Sometimes, an Amazonian woman is just what you need to keep you happier!!!

152. The Modern Day is what we're living in…

151. I'm almost done with this book: time to break open a bottle of Champagne!!!

150. May as well throw in a hundred luft balloons…

149. I want to thank you for reading this far along w/ my book

148. What is tomorrow going to be like??? More of the same or something different: sometimes, something different is what you need to keep you occupied.

147. Do machines really dehumanize people??? Not really: but, they do take jobs away from people so that greedy corporations can get wealthier and pay no taxes: what's up with that???!!!

146. When a machine really comes apart it's not a pretty sight to see…

145. Just because the house is glass doesn't mean that you need to throw a rock at it to ruin it. How would you feel if somebody did that to you???!!!

144. Sometimes a math equation is the best thing you can solve: you don't need to be GENUIS to solve a math problem. Just take your time when doing it.

143. **The Devil Made Me Do It**: really???!!! It wasn't the Devil, it was you…

142. Sometimes you don't want to talk things out: you just want to get the 'F out of Dodge!!!

141. No matter what happens make sure that you laugh your butt off 50++ times per day. You'll thank me later…much later…

140. Time heals all wounds: thank God time can also wound all heals…

139. Stop Making Sense

138. A really cold bath might just be what the doctor ordered.

137. You can always go fishing any time of the year!!!

136. Make sure that you get a good pitchfork to dig up some night crawlers before you go fishing for the day.

135. Love Is In The Air at all times of the day & night: sometimes it's just hard to feel it because you are too wrapped up in your thoughts.

134. I Feel Love: I FEEL LOVE!!!

133. I SPECIALIZE in making people happy: before you can do that make sure that your heart is in the right place…

132. What really was 'The Cold War' anyways???

131. When somebody knocks on your door you don't have to answer it especially when you know who it is…or, you can answer it: that's all up to you.

130. Bigger Ain't Necessarily Better!!!

129. Sometimes, it's best to have FFUN with the quietest person on the room.

128. Ain't No Mountain High Enough

127. Talk, Talk: sometimes that's all anybody wants to or needs to do: just let them talk and then walk away when the time is right!

126. Sometimes, interrupting a person when they are venting just won't do. Let 'em keep talking so they can get it all out even if it does bore you.

125. Sometimes, walking away from somebody who is venting will cause more grief later on down the line. That person really needs you to hear what they have to say.

124. Sometimes, thinking that something is going to work out will not work with you: time to move on.

123. If the Great Wall didn't work in Asia why does Trump think that building a Wall here in America will work???

122. My favorite meal as a child was cheese sandwiches & tomato soup: what was your favorite meal: you can always eat 'Comfort Food' in order to calm yourself down…

123. When all hope is gone there is a whole full heart full of more HOPE!!!

122. Which is better: lonely vs alone: I'd prefer to be ALONE vs. lonely: I can always touch my elf! I don't need to be with people all the time: I can get used to the idea of being ALONE and not lonely (pining away for somebody to be in my life).

121. I used to think I was going to become very famous: how wrong I was: now that I'm much older and a little bit wiser, I'm o.k. with where my life has taken me so far…

120. The **EGO** is the hardest thing to tame with a person. You might want to tame it or you might want to let it get out of control: depends on the situation.

119. Letting Go is sometimes the very best thing you can do…who's to stop you??? The ultimate letting go is death.

118. What is there to really worry about these days??? NOTHING!!!

117. Don't Let It End: don't let what end: with everything in life there are 5 parts: preparation, memorization, more preparation, the opening night & then the finale: make sure that you don't break a leg on your 1st night.

116. I Will Always Love You

115. There's a place and a time for everything with your life: just go with the flow…

114. Sometimes going against the flow is what you really want: go against the tides that are coming in and get outta there as quickly as you can: you don't need **THAT**!!!

113. When in doubt ride a rollercoaster all day long or just get your butt to the Rollercoaster Park in Jackson, NJ

112. When the rollercoaster park isn't open you can always go to the water park and have a great time doing it: just make sure that you don't go 2 days in a row: the bleach in the water might just make you sick if you're a sensitive person.

111. You can always grow a tomato plant in the dead of winter: just make sure that you give the plant enough water, nutrition and sunlight to get it to grow and produce tomatoes!!!

110. A trip all the way across America is a great thing to do especially when you go with somebody that you love…

109. I asked a friend why he does the things he does and he said, "Because I can." When he was drinking he'd do mean things just to make a point: I didn't like it but his actions made me like him even less.

108. The Way You Do The Things You Do: that's my kinda person!

107. Just because you are in a sour mood doesn't mean that you need to get upset and start running your mouth: maybe it's time to just be QUIET & learn something from being QUIET about the way you feel???!!! But, if you can't be quiet then you may as well vent to get it out of your system.

106. If you could live anywhere but America where would it be: make plans and just pick up & go when the time is right: don't forget your cell phone and all of your legal documents!!!

105. Twisted vs. Sick: if somebody calls you sick they're acting like there's a CURE. Just correct them and say, "I'm just a little bit TWISTED like my Twisted Sister." What can they possibly say???

104. Sometimes the best thing you can do is eat a whole box of something by yourself like chocolates, cereal or a gallon of ice cream!!! Just don't do it all the time.

103. If you can count all the way to 100 then you'll have no problem counting all the way to a 1000.

102. How many times can you jump on a Pogo Stick to break The Guinness Book of World Records???!!! That task requires a lot of effort and eventually you'll fall off the pogo stick whether you like it or not.

101. Being OVERLOADED means that maybe you should just stop making commitments that you don't need to be making???!!!

100. Find One Hundred Ways to get the job done: it took Edison more than 100 times to perfect the lightbulb…

99. Take a really cold bath if you want to really chill out

98. Sometimes, you'll be at a loss for words and there's nothing you'll need to do about it: just accept that there are no words to describe what you are going through.

97. TAKE A BREAK: eat a Kit Katt Bar then go right back to what you need to finish…

96. The Longest Yard is a movie about what??? Be grateful that you know what a YARD is…for those who don't know it's 3 feet.

95. Help Me Make It Through The Night

94. You can be anybody that you'd like to be: go quietly in the night…

93. All Through The Night I'll be there waiting for you…

92. What really is SNOWBLIND

91. You can run but you can't hide from your EMOTIONS: be glad that God/Goddess/Godhead gave you something to work with. Some people have less than you have, other people have more than you have: just be grateful for what you have.

90. What really is **WHITEPAPER**???!!!

89. Sometimes, it's great to have a closer circle of friends that you can rely on.

88. We Are The Champions

87. When in doubt don't start worrying about what will happen: just be glad that you can still think.

86. Being THANKFUL sometimes just won't do: or, will it??? THANKFUL!!!

85. Make something of the ashes of your life: there will be many opportunities left to express yourself!!!

84. Sometimes, the best thing you can do is go to a party with somebody and have a great time with the new people you meet at the party!!!

83. Let The Sunshine In let the sun shine in...let the sun shine IN...

82. The older you get the more there is No Room For Sorrow.

81. What are cryptic messages anyways???

80. Sometimes, people pass through your life like Ships In The Night: be glad that that's all it is...

79. Spread Your Wings and enfold the whole human race!

78. Who doesn't know what a 78 RPM, 33 1/3 RPM really is and that thingamajig in the middle of the 45 is used for???!!!

77. What was your favorite year for Pop Muzik: maybe you should revisit some of those songs online or even in your 45 RPM Collection: have FFUN listening to those tunes…

76. The Spirit of '76

75. Sometimes the very thing that you need to say is I QUIT but make sure that you really want to do it…

74. You just got your computer back from the repair shop and now it runs even faster than ever!!! Woo-hoo!!! Woo-hoo!!!

73. You're the richest man on the Planet: at least in your mind!

72. You're the richest woman on the Planet: at least in your dreams!

71. "Keep Your Feet On The Ground &Keep Reaching For The Stars" – Casey Kasem

70. Even though there is snow on the ground it feels like a warm Spring Day with all that melting going on: what's up with that???!!!

69. Your favorite Number in the world is 69: well, that's my favorite #. What really IS your favorite number???!!!

68. If birds have wings then they might be able to fly. If you had wings then you'd be able to fly, too!!! Birds find small edible creatures underneath leaves & snow like insects, spiders, grubs. They also eat seeds, grains and berries, worms,

67. The Indians gave their lives so that you can live in this Country. Give thanks.

66. It's THANKSGIVING…AGAIN!

65. America was not founded by Christopher Columbus, it was really founded by…Leif Eriksson 500 years before Columbus.

64. You're not living in Africa and you won't starve to death anytime soon so quit your beatching!!!

63. That you were sometimes called to dinner by a dinner bell when you were a child in Northern Maine.

62. That you can always start studying something new at any age!!!

61. We Are The World, We are the children, we are the ones who make a brighter day so let's start giving, there's a choice we're making, we're saving our own lives, so let's start giving…remember: only 17%A of what was raised in 1984 was given to the children. The other 83% was used to run the organization that raised all that money to help the Children of The World.

60. You are beautiful at any age

59. Spring will be here in 29 Days: something to be thankful for

58. The Birds & The Bees: thanks be to God that your mother & father never explained that one to you! You already knew about that kind of stuff from all the small talk you heard while growing up.

57. 57 Channels And Nothin' On

56. That 56 comes before 57…

55. A pentaphobe is somebody who fears the #5: what's up with that??? I don't!!!

54. The Love You Give Is Equal To The Love You Make

53. Just because you haven't been to church in several years doesn't mean that you can't go back to church to receive the Communion of God & Jesus!!! If that's what you want to do: Take Me To The River, dip me in the water, washing me down, washing me down…

52. You've made it this far you are to be commended!!!

51. 51/50 is a great place to STOP!

50. Can you imagine making it all the way to 50 years of age??? Be glad that you are living your life.

49. You can choose to like and love your self. You really CAN!!!

48. When somebody gives you a compliment don't just stand there and act all dumbfounded: ACCEPT THE COMPLIMENT WITH A LITTLE BIT OF HUMILITY, COMPASSION or LOVE! That's what you are supposed to do when somebody is being genuine. Even if they're being sarcastic accept the compliment: it flew out of their mouth. Don't take how they said it personally.

47. This is going to be THE BEST DAY OF YOUR LIFE!

46. You have all your life to discover who you are!

45. Where would you be without love???

44. 4 + 4 = 8: the symbol of returns is on YOU, sweet wonderful YOU!!!

43. Be Happy No Matter What: make that decision in your head and don't let anything or anyone bother you.

42. Where would you be without your Negative Thoughts & Emotions that bring you down??? Much better off!!!

41. Hell IS Your Thoughts so why not **RAISE YOUR VIBRATIONS TO A MUCH HIGHER LEVEL**!!!

40. There's always a pot of gold at the End of The Rainbow

39. The Rainbow Connection

38. When You Wish Upon A Star your dreams will come true!!!

37. You can choose to like who you like

36. You can choose to ignore everybody

35. You can choose to like nobody if that's the way you feel

34. You can sleep as long as you need to in order to feel rested. If you're that exhausted then you might want to consider exercise to get that energy back, eating healthy food and being around people who support your being and becoming.

33. They say a half hour of exercise a day is best for the human body to maintain optimal health: do some exercise regularly. At the very least you can go walking for 20-30 minutes a day twice a day or do Yoga (stretching exercises) to keep yourself limber.

32. The healthier you eat the better off you are: Vegetarianism is recommended but you need to make sure that you get your intake of B Vitamins. Meat is the hardest to digest. Fruits, Vegetables & Grains are the healthiest option for your body but what you eat is all up to you. Trust your body on an intuitive level. What do you really need to keep your body happy??? Stay away from white processed products: flour, dairy and sugar. Eat Natural vs Processed Sugars that rot your teeth, make you gain weight, make you high, etc.

31. Meditate at least 20-30 minutes twice a day. At the very least for 5 minutes when you wake up in the morning & 5 minutes at night before you go to bed. It's just a place to calm down, chill out and reflect about the past, and what happened during the day, etc.

30. You are in control of your **Destiny**: what do you really need in your life to make and keep you happy.

29. Read any book by Byron Katie: 'I Need Your Love: Is That True' or 'Loving What Is': do "The Work" in the book to clear up old emotional problems and understand your self-better!!!

28. Stay away from people who drain your energy and your resources: they're just takers: as soon as they get what they want they'll be gone never to be heard from again. People usually want you for only **4 reasons**: **1.** To borrow money and not pay it back. **2.** To borrow something they don't return. **3.** To talk you ears off. **4.** Any other reason. Develop Boundaries and learn to say, "NO," & "Go Love Your Self." If the person takes it the wrong way just tell them: that's not how I meant it but if that's the way you understand it...

27. Listen to your "Inner Gut Feelings" or the "Little Voice Inside Your Head". It will protect you from bad things happening and protect your heart: you don't owe anybody anything except the contracts you make with people that are usually invisible. Write contracts with everybody and make sure that you create WIN/ **Situations** in your life: that's why you are here: you're not here to be taken advantage of, walked all over and treated like shirt. Develop boundaries with people. That prevents the shirt from hitting the fan.

26. Get rid of anything you haven't used in 6 months to a year: give it away, sell it at a Yard Sale, give it to somebody who needs it, throw junk and garbage out.

25. When you need help from somebody ask for it: the most they can say is, "No." Learn the meaning of asking for help and taking care of you. You will be better off making your life the best life you can make it be by surrounding yourself with people who love you and that you love, not people who take advantage of you because they know they can and will.

24. When you need to take a break from what you are doing go for it.

23. Keep an Inventory of everything you own. Any negative behaviors you learned as a child you have to come to terms with. Don't become a hoarder, bully, verbal abuser, drama queen, etc.

22. Buy yourself a pet to take care of and really take care of the animal: they need your love as much as you need their love. Make sure that you have a book or manual so that you can read up about the proper care of your pet. The smaller the pet is the harder it is going to be to take care of them.

21. If you need to go to a "Self-Help Group" regularly then do it: anything that works to help your sense of self-esteem: AA, ACOA, NA, FA, Spiritual Groups, etc. Anything!!!

20. Join a Club if that's your thing or start your own club.

19. Put together model airplanes, trains, cars, etc. Anything that clears your mind as a hobby is good to do for you.

18. Just sitting down and observing people, places & things is a good thing to do without saying anything.

17. Keep your friends close and your enemies even closer: don't let people walk all over you: that's not why we are here.

16. If you need medications for mental health problems seek Alternatives, not Big Pharma.

15. Which do you prefer to eat: Organic vs Natural Foods produced with chemicals: its' your choice but remember: your mind, body, soul and spirit pay for your decisions. So what 'Organic Food' costs twice as much: it's worth every penny even though the food with chemicals in it should cost twice as much as it really is crap.

14. Call people to talk to when you need to but don't become a nuisance.

13. Go back to college if you need do. If you are in High School and don't know if you want to go to college, graduate and then take 2 years off and then make a decision to go back to school when you are ready to do so. A job is much better than being in school for X amount of years and getting a useless degree and having to pay back those expensive college loans that are going to balloon into an expensive debt because of the high interest rate.

12. Breathing fresh air from outside every day is very good to do.

11. Get rid of all Bad Habits. You don't need them. Eliminate them gradually.

10. Love Your Self like no other person can. You don't need to love other people as much as you need to love yourself.

09. Just because somebody doesn't love you the way you want to be loved doesn't mean that they don't love you: they'll speak to you when they want to: otherwise, why make a big deal out of it???

08. When in doubt or angry about a situation take a break and never make decisions in the heat of the moment or when you're angry as you might make the wrong decision: the goal is to keep yourself healthy, happy & alive, not screwed up emotionally. You know what somebody's vibrations are before you even become their friend: don't buy into their crap. You don't need that.

07. Take a hot bath with whatever you need to put in the bath water to reduce the tension in your body and keep you clean: lavender, lemon, sea salt, clay, bubble bath, bath bombs, etc.

06. There is a whole wide world out there: what do you really want to see and do: make plans to do that.

05. Just because you have a medical problems or medical conditions: don't let that get in the way of living your life: work with what you've got and the lessons having those medical problems or conditions gives you.

04. There are more things in the world than one knows what to do with: what do you want or need and how do you want to live your life: live your life the way you need to live your life, not the way people tell you to live your life: there is a difference.

03. Take a good long hard look in the mirror: it's all on you: praise yourself as much as you need to, say the words you need to say to encourage you, SMILE, etc. You are the one in charge of your ship, not

other people who feel the need to direct you and drain you of your energy and resources.

02. Don't hang around people who think it's their duty to change you: change yourself for you, not anybody else. Take only the Advice people give you that you need and throw the rest of the Advice out!!! You don't need that!!! And, you don't need to help people unless they need and ask for your help. Sometimes, it's best to just step on your lips no matter what: let the person figure things out on their own.

01. Peace, Love, Prosperity, Laughter, Light & Joy is what we are here for: let's make ourselves better in the long run & forget about the rest: Namaste: I honor the Spirit & Soul that is sweet, wonderful YOU: Go Now, Make a Wonderful Life For Your Self!!! STOP! kissing other people's a**e*...you don't need to be doing that!!! **JUST STOP! DOING IT!!!**

goherenextoday.blogspot.com thru blogspot.com/Google: Get your BONUS TODAY:
ashleylenartson@gmail.com Go Now...

www.ingramcontent.com/pod-product-compliance
Lightning Source LLC
Chambersburg PA
CBHW080930260726
48661CB00010B/3863